Youth Programs:
Promoting Quality Services

Susan R. Edginton
Christopher R. Edginton

SAGAMORE PUBLISHING
Champaign, IL

Production Manager: Susan M. McKinney
Cover Design: Michelle R. Dressen
Proofreader: Phyllis L. Bannon

ISBN: 0-915611-97-x
Library of Congress Catalog Card Number:94-65747

Printed in the United States

10 9 8 7 6

To Carole and David Edginton

Contents

Preface

Youth Programs: Promoting Quality Services has been prepared to assist youth leaders in creating and implementing programs and activities that are innovative, dynamic, and that have a core of youth development principles. This book contains the information needed to operate high-caliber, high-impact youth programs. It includes materials on such topics as youth development, program planning, program evaluation, risk management, behavior management, leadership, customer service, public relations and youth development.

Some of the concepts related to youth development may be new to youth leaders, and it is important that leaders providing services to youth become familiar with these guidelines. The insertion of youth development competencies (developmental experiences for youth) into leisure (nonschool) programs and services will help youth reach their potential and become positive, productive adults able to cope with life challenges.

There are a number of national trends impacting on youth today that reinforce the need for strong, well-managed youth programs in our communities. Many of these issues are troubling. It is important for you, as a youth leader, to consider the ways in which youth programs and services can have a preventative or prescriptive impact on youth. The way in which young people meet their basic needs and develop as individuals will be impacted by individuals, organizations and agencies that influence their lives. Youth leaders play such a role.

We express appreciation for the support needed to produce these materials. Some of the individuals who have contributed their ideas and support toward the development of this effort are Robert Harding, Keith Painter and Jane Wilde. Other individuals who contributed to the book, are Dr. Don DeGraaf, Kathy DeGraaf, Dr. Debra Jordan, Lou Tanselli, David Edginton, Carole Edginton and Dr. Susan Koch. We extend our appreciation to them.

Susan R. Edginton
Christopher R. Edginton, Ph.D.

INTRODUCTION

YOUTH PROGRAMS: PROMOTING QUALITY SERVICES

As North American society has evolved over the last two decades, it has changed the way in which youth live their lives. Today's youth need a more rigorous social support system during non-school hours. They require leadership, programs, and services that will enable them to gain life skills, help them to develop strong values, make educated and positive choices, and operate in an independent manner. Issues related to sense of community in a more transient society, more nontraditional families, less direct parenting after school and conflicting societal values not only affect youth, but have implications for youth-serving organizations. There is a strong need today for youth leaders to possess knowledge of factors underlying youth development and to consider the role of leisure service and youth-serving organizations in helping youth operate effectively in contemporary society.

Youth development programs are provided by a number of agencies and organizations in the United States and Canada. Organizations such as the Boys and Girls Clubs of America, Boy Scouts of America, Girls Scouts of the U.S.A., Girls, Inc., Camp Fire Boys and Girls, Big Brothers/Big Sisters of America, *Camp Adventure*™, Junior Achievement, National 4-H Clubs, The Salvation Army, American Red Cross, non-profit sports associations, YMCA's and YWCA's, fraternal organizations, churches, U.S. military morale, welfare and recreation units, and municipal and county parks and recreation departments all plan, organize and implement youth programs and services.

This book is designed to assist youth leaders in providing comprehensive youth programs. Emphasis will be placed upon youth development concepts which suggest that youth programs should provide activities which promote and foster social interaction, personal growth, leisure skills and educational opportunities. The following will be emphasized.

▶   Promotion of quality services with an emphasis on the process known as Total Quality Program Planning (TQP).

▶   Youth development principles, pursuits and activities which promote the development and acquisition of lifelong skills, leading to physical, social, cultural, emotional, psychological, mental and spiritual well-being.

▶   The process of values development, values clarification as well as the impact of values within youth programs.

▶   A program planning process that includes opportunities for youth leadership and involvement.

The information in the book will assist the youth leader in addressing these issues.

Time Use and Youth

In a landmark report, commissioned and published by the Carnegie Corporation of New York entitled *A Matter of Time: Risk and Opportunity in the Nonschool Hours*, the authors and contributors note the following.

All Americans have a vital stake in the healthy development of today's young adolescents, who will become tomorrow's parents, workers, and citizens. But millions of America's young adolescents are not developing into responsible members of society. Many likely will not lead productive or fulfilling lives. . . . They are profoundly influenced by experiences in their neighborhoods and the larger community during nonschool hours (Carnegie Corporation, 1992:9).

As youth move through childhood and adolescence they are faced with many challenges. This is a time when values are formed and life interests shaped. It is a time of great exploration and, in general, a time when preparation for adulthood begins in earnest. Also it is a time during which youth face many challenges and risks. The passage from adolescence to adulthood can be eased by the support of carefully crafted programs and services directed toward the development, enhancement and enrichment of youth. One of the major challenges faced by youth is the productive use of their nonschool hours.

How do youth spend their time? Timmer, Eccles, and O'Brian (1985) report that the majority of time spent by youth is discretionary time. They note that 42 percent of the average youth's day is spent engaged is what could be defined as leisure time, involved in such activities as television watching, playing, hobbies, art activities, sports and outdoor activities, attending church and visiting friends. This can be compared with 31.7 percent of their time that is spent in school-related activities.

Many youth spend much of their leisure time in nonstructured activities without adult supervision. They are often left to their own devices to create meaningful and relevant experiences that contribute to their development in a positive manner. Unfortunately, increasingly many youth choose to participate in activities that place them at risk. Such behavior serves as an indicator of the need to create more effectively organized use of nonschool hours.

Why Leisure Programs for Youth?

Participation in high-quality, creative and meaningful programs is a high priority for youth. This book is focused on creating and delivering youth services with excellence. Following are benefits to youth of participation in well-organized developmentally sound youth programs:

❏   **Personal development.** Improved self-concept, sense of achievement, spiritual growth, enhanced creativity, learning, self-reliance.

❏   **Social growth.** Acquire new friends, learn group skills, gain social support and enjoy family togetherness.

❏   **Physical development.** Enhanced physical fitness and wellness, development of motor skills, better energy level, greater stamina, improved self-image and better coordination.

❏   **Improved psychological health.** Enhanced sense of well-being occurs since recreation activities are designed to produce positive personal outcomes. Opportunities for experiencing a sense of independence and freedom

❏   **Acquire positive values.** Acquire new positive *values* or strengthen existing values, through teamwork, cooperation, learning and interacting with positive role models.

❏   **Self-expression.** Opportunities for self-expression, creativity, supervised risk, fantasy, progression toward personal potential.

❏   **Learning and growth.** Opportunities for learning and growth, exploration and exposure to new facts and ideas. Activities that enhance appreciation of nature, the arts, science and other topics.

❏   **Memories, inner resources.** A chance for youth to build within themselves a wealth of positive, pleasant, magic memories that will strengthen and sustain them through their childhood and adulthood.

It is evident that there are many benefits to youth that may occur as a result of involvement in youth programs and activities.

What You Will Learn

As you progress through this book you will acquire the knowledge necessary to provide an effective, dynamic youth development program. You will learn practical skills and techniques to help you plan and carry out programs, as well as values that touch the intangible aspects of working with youth. The information you learn will help you make your organization a more progressive, fun and challenging place for youth.

In order to introduce you to the material that will be covered in this book a brief description of each of the sections is offered: Part I — Total Quality Program Planning; Part II — Youth Development; and Part III — Youth-Centered Program Planning.   This material will provide you with information regarding the theory, values and practical applications that are important in the provision of youth services.

Part I of the book is focused on the topic of "Total Quality Program Planning"(TQP). Although later sections in this book will assist you in creating programs that are *technically* correct, high quality youth programs have something more, *something extra*.   Total Quality Program Planning (TQP) involves going beyond the provision of simply adequate programs.   The youth leader involved in TQP (Total Quality Program Planning) is committed to creating services that exceed the expectations of youth, their parents and the community.

Also discussed in Part I are the actions necessary to produce "programs with a high degree of excellence," as opposed to average ones. It covers topics such as: creating "magic" programs for youth, in terms of a vision for the program, creating the environment and connecting with youth. It also discusses commitment to quality and customer service. In addition, this section includes a TQP Checklist; that is, a checklist that the leader may use as a guide in providing high-caliber "Total Quality Program Planning."

"Youth Development" is the focus of Part II of the book. As a youth leader, you will have an impact upon the development of the youth you serve. The programs and services you select, and the way that you interact with youth will impact upon their *physical, social, intellectual, emotional and psychological development*. This section will help you gain an understanding of: the importance of youth development, including values and issues; knowledge of the stages of youth development, the competencies/ skills that youth should acquire; and the importance of promoting positive values in programming, as well as encouragement of youth leadership.

More specifically, in Part II you will gain an understanding of how to modify programs to meet the needs of different age groups, as well as methods for integrating youth development competencies into programming, including health/physical competencies, personal/social competencies, cognitive/creative competencies, vocational competencies and citizenship and ethics competencies. Knowledge in these areas will help you to enrich your programs, as well as help you to assist youth in reaching their potential as individuals.

The last section of the book, Part III, is entitled "Youth-Centered Program Design." This section of the book will present a diagram of the program planning process, and then guide you through each of the steps of the planning process in sequence. It will give insight into the process of assessing the needs of youth, promoting involvement of youth and program development and implementation.

Part III will help you to: plan programs that have appeal to youth, based on current trends, youth needs and interests; develop program goals and objectives; select a program format, manage the program flow; and evaluate programs. You will learn how to develop program offerings in a way that allows youth freedom within structure, that offers them opportunities for leadership and influence, and that are based on sound principles of supervision, risk management and behavior management.

References

Carnegie Council on Adolescent Development — Task Force on Youth Development and Community Programs (1992). *A Matter of Time: Risk and Opportunity in the Nonschool Hours.* New York: Carnegie Corporation of New York.

Timmer, S.G., J. Eccles, & I. O'Brian (1985). In F.T. Juster and F.B. Stafford (Eds.), *Time, Goods and Well-Being.* Ann Arbor: University of Michigan, Institute for Social Research.

PART I

TOTAL QUALITY PROGRAM PLANNING (TQP)

CHAPTER 1

COMMITMENT TO QUALITY

Individuals and organizations that focus their efforts on quality will outperform those focused elsewhere. The provision of high-quality youth services is an individual responsibility, as well as an organizational one. Quality is an attitude that results in superior performance. It results from the efforts of a youth leader who is committed, dedicated, and takes pride in producing services of the highest caliber for youth.

This chapter will provide an overview of Total Quality Program Planning (Edginton & Edginton,1993). The youth leader involved in Total Quality Program Planning (TQP) creates services that exceed the expectations of youth, their parents and the community. The TQP approach includes commitment to quality, effective planning, creating "magic" for youth, helping youth feel valued, and encouraging youth development, involvement and leadership.

As a result of reading this chapter, you will be able to:

▶ Understand Total Quality Program Planning, and what action is required by the leader to produce high-quality programs.

▶ Appreciate the importance of striving for excellence, and using standards to meet this goal.

▶ Gain an understanding of the methods that can be used to produce programs that exceed youths' expectations.

MAKING A COMMITMENT TO QUALITY

The youth leader involved ih Total Quality Program Planning (TQP) uses guidelines to create services that exceed the expectations of youth. There are many well-funded, wonderful facilities, staffed with capable professionals that don't attract youth, or that produce an uninspiring program of activities for those youth who do attend. The goal of the youth leader is not only to produce a technically and developmentally sound program, but to create a special intangible quality within the program or event that touches the emotional or spiritual side of youth.

What is Quality?

What is quality? Quality is difficult to define, but . . . you know it when you see it! Quality is not just measured by numbers of participants or meeting the break-even cost of a program; it is also measured in the reaction of participants, the way in which a program unfolds, the degree to which youth develop and meet their needs, and the extent to which youth genuinely, enthusiastically and meaningfully experience leisure.

The Total Quality Program Planning (TQP) process is based on the assumption that the leader can work within the organization to produce quality leisure programs that consistently and effectively meet the needs of youth, and even exceed their expectations. Organizations and leaders committed to the concept of quality will outperform those that are not.

Quality is often thought of as a perception of "excellence." It is an attitude that leaders have that transforms their effort into purposeful, meaningful, and creative leisure programs. Quality performance requires a focus on the needs of the customer (youth, parents and community) as the cornerstone for creating services that are relevant and that help youth feel valued.

How Do You Measure Quality?

Quality is not something that is measured in terms of "good" or "bad." Rather, quality is usually described as whether the organization achieves the requirements that have been established for serving youth. Quality, then is the conformance to requirements, standards, or policies or procedures. Such standards and requirements present guidelines to assist the youth leader in meeting the minimum expectations for programs.

However, it is important to remember that standards or requirements are often written only in terms of the *minimal levels* of achievement or expectation. Total Quality Program Planning is directed toward *exceeding expectations*; constantly improving not only upon the impact of programs, but also the processes that are used to produce them.

The achievement of quality can be measured quantitatively. Youth leaders can determine the extent to which they successfully achieve organizational requirements and, then, improve the delivery of services.

Your Role as a Youth Leader

Commitment to quality requires the youth leader to find better ways to serve youth. It involves a commitment to creating "better" youth services by working in a way that leads to innovation, reduction of mistakes, positiveness, attention to detail, and other factors. Commitment to quality requires youth leaders to constantly improve their expertise and knowledge through continuous development.

The goal of the youth leader who uses Total Quality Program Planning is to produce not only a technically and developmentally sound program of events, but to create programs that *exceed minimum requirements*; that is, programs that create a special intangible, "magic," quality that inspires youth, provides heightened insight, introspection, development, and is meaningful.

In this sense, Total Quality Program Planning is dedicated to producing magic moments for children and youth that last a lifetime. A quality program will produce positive experiences for youth that they will carry with them throughout their childhood and adult life. Such experiences will be locked into the minds and emotions of youth and serve as a beacon for future positive adult behaviors. However, these types of experiences can only be produced when the focus of the leadership within the organization is on the creation of quality programs that incorporate youth development and that use a youth-centered program design.

Your Role as a Youth Leader:
How to Plan "Total Quality" Programs

1. Strive to Achieve Hallmarks of Quality

2. Create Programs That Are "Magic" for Youth

3. Give Excellence in Customer Service

4. Use a Foundation of Youth Development

5. Use a Youth-Centered Program Design

HALLMARKS OF QUALITY: GUIDELINES FOR THE YOUTH LEADER

It is the responsibility of the youth leader to build program efforts around the idea of commitment to quality. A focus on quality must be evident throughout the organization and as a major focus of the organization. Youth Leaders must work toward *eliminating* poorly organized services, poor attitudes toward youth, use of poor equipment/materials and willingness to live with mediocrity.

A philosophy of excellence that focuses on high quality programs and services should be applied vigorously in the area of youth services. The hallmarks of quality (or guidelines) for organizations that are committed to quality are best reflected in the following statements.

❑ Innovation

❑ Future orientation

❑ Getting things right
   the first time

❑ Constant improvement

❑ Continuous improvement

❑ Attention to detail

❑ Pride/belief in service

❑ Anticipatory planning

❑ Performance
   measurements

❑ Elimination of mistakes

❑ Elimination of
   negativisim

❑ Personal responsibility

❑ Teaming: Doing what it takes

These hallmarks or guidelines of quality, that are used by organizations and leaders with a strong commitment to quality are discussed more fully below (Walton, 1988:34-36).

❑   **Innovation.** Success in youth programming stems from a commitment to innovation. No program should be the same from one year to the next. Programs should constantly evolve to meet the changing needs of children and youth. Innovative organizations are constantly looking for new and different services, equipment, areas and facilities that improve the quality of services to youth.

❏ **Future Orientation.** Youth leaders who not only address quality issues of today, but those of tomorrow will be successful. It is important that you include in your work not only the *immediate* needs of your organization for quality, but some focus on what can be done in the future to promote quality. Youth service organizations that invest in the future invest some of their resources in ensuring that their programs and services are successful and vibrant in months and years to come.

❏ **Getting Things Right the First Time.** Perhaps the most efficient way to promote quality within your organization is to do things right the first time. Sloppiness and a "seat of the pants," last-minute approach to planning often lead to having to redo activities or services. This is not only costly, but results in poor performance. Some activities and programs cannot be corrected if they are not planned effectively, and the opportunity they presented for youth is lost.

❏ **Continuous Improvement.** The best way to achieve quality is to improve the processes associated with creating youth services. The job of any youth leader should be to find ways to continuously improve upon programs and services. Constantly searching out new ways of doing things better, more cost efficiently and/or in a way that is more meaningful to youth. Establish a goal of making one small change in every program every week to improve the quality. This is a never-ending dynamic process. It should not be thought of as a one-time event.

☐ **Continuous Education.** The continuous development of the youth leader in terms of knowledge and skill is essential to achieving quality. Good people make good programs, but the needs of youth are dynamic and changing, requiring continuous education and development. Youth leaders should seek ways to improve their knowledge base.

☐ **Attention to Detail.** Success in youth programs is painted in small steps as well as broad strokes. The little things that you do to make a program of high quality, make the difference between superior services and mediocre ones.

☐ **Pride.** Belief in what you are doing is contagious. Pride is having a high opinion of yourself and your work. Pride comes from doing a job competently as well as having ownership in the effort.

☐ **Anticipatory Planning.** Don't merely respond to the needs of youth as they are expressed from moment to moment. Learn how to anticipate needs in advance and meet them before they are requested. Anticipatory planning requires the leader to think in advance (days, weeks months) and to visualize services as they will likely unfold, and anticipate actions that may be needed.

☐ **Performance Measurements.** Find ways to record your progress toward achieving quality by creating performance measurements. Determine how to chart your progress toward the achievement of quality. Graphs and charts provide opportunities for discussion, focus on opportunities for change, and may lead to the development of new programs and/or better methods and procedures.

Participant number, youth outcomes related to performance measures, program costs, participant use hours, participant survey results are all sources of data for charts to measure performance. Measuring achievement over a period of time, enables the youth leader to see the gains in quality and performance, and possibly to justify future program developments.

❑   **Elimination of Mistakes.** Mistakes are costly to an organization both in terms of funds and image. Mistakes made in program planning are costly to participants in terms of opportunity for development. *If play/leisure is powerful enough to help youth it is powerful enough to hurt them.* When mistakes in program planning impact on the quality of services, they also impact on youth. Eliminating mistakes helps improve quality, morale, cost effectiveness and other critical factors.

❑   **Elimination of Negativeness.** Positive attitudes are important in the delivery of youth services. Youth leaders should strive to be enthusiastic, energetic and zestful. If you enjoy what you are doing, that quality will rub off on others; the reverse is also true. Positiveness is a "can do" attitude that promotes a willingness to find ways to effectively serve youth with quality programs.

❑   **Assume Personal Responsibility for Quality.** The old way to get quality was to supervise and inspect services and manage change from the top down, or from without. The new way of promoting quality is to build it from within. The best way to promote quality from within is to ensure that *each individual* assumes personal responsibility and accountability for making sure that services are provided in an excellent, high-quality manner.

☐ **Teaming: Doing What It Takes To Get the Job Done.** The youth leader as well as other staff must be willing to do what it takes to get the job done, and to get it done right. The Total Quality approach, is dependent upon teamwork, cooperation and supportive behavior. It is not "your job" or "my job" but, rather, "our job." All staff should be focused and have their eyes and efforts directed toward the *primary goal*, that is providing the very highest quality services for youth, and they should be willing to do what it takes to make that happen.

The committed leader who attempts to produce quality programs will have a more positive impact upon youth.

Hallmarks of Quality in Program Planning

☆ Innovation   ☆ Pride/Belief in service

☆ Future orientation   ☆ Planning Ahead

☆ Getting things right the first time ☆ Performance measurements

☆ Constant improvement   ☆ Elimination of mistakes

☆ Continuous improvement   ☆ Elimination of negativism

☆ Attention to detail   ☆ Personal responsibility

☆ Teaming: Doing what it takes

A Final Note

Youth service organizations that strive for excellence will outproduce those that are focused elsewhere. Excellence is an attitude; an attitude that promotes concern for producing quality services that exceed the expectations of youth.

Personal Notes: Commitment to Quality

Review the action steps that indicate a commitment to quality that were presented in this chapter. Based upon past experiences and your knowledge of your own strengths, which of these statements pertains to you and the strengths that you will bring to your organization? Please list them.

❑ Innovation   ❑ Pride /belief in service
❑ Future orientation   ❑ Anticipatory planning
❑ Getting things right   ❑ Performance measurements
   the first time   ❑ Constant improvement
❑ Elimination of mistakes   ❑ Continuous improvement
❑ Elimination of negativism   ❑ Attention to detail
❑ Personal responsibility   ❑ Teaming: Doing what it takes

_____   _____

_____   _____

_____   _____

_____   _____

_____   _____

The statements that you mention above will be strengths that you will bring to your work as a youth services leader and will strengthen your programs. Now, which of the previous action step statements do *not* pertain to you and will challenge you? Which ones offer you new information that will present you with an opportunity to develop yourself so that you have a total commitment to quality? Please list them.

References

Edginton, C.R. and S.R. Edginton (1993). Total Quality Programming Planning. *Journal of Physical Education, Recreation and Dance 64* (8) p.40-42, 47.

Walton, M. (1988). *The Deming Management Model*. New York: Perigee.

CHAPTER 2

CREATING MAGIC FOR YOUTH

How does the youth leader produce those special, magic moments that create memories for youth that last a lifetime? Creating magic for youth is a challenge and opportunity of youth leaders. We can all remember a youth leader who made a difference in our lives, who connected with us in a positive way that greatly influenced our development and our view of life. Such positive experiences are imprinted into our memories and serve as beacons to guide future positive behaviors. Magic moments are those special experiences that shape who we are, our values, our sense of self-esteem, our sense of self-worth, and how we relate to others.

In this chapter, we will present a set of *steps for producing "magic" moments* within recreation programs and activities (Edginton and Edginton, 1992). Magic moments occur when youth feel competent, a sense of belonging, a sense of achievement and a sense of freedom and influence. Youth leaders can consistently produce dynamic, energetic and meaningful programs and activities for youth by following the guidelines presented in this section of the book.

As a result of reading this chapter, you will be able to:

▶ Understand the need to create a vision for programs and events.

▶ Structure programs and events in order to create a mood, an illusion and a sense of expectation.

▶ Increase the impact of programming by planning opportunities for youth for personal contact and recognition.

CREATING MAGIC

The goal of the youth leader is not only to produce a technically and developmentally sound program or event, but to create a special quality within the program or event that touches the emotional/spiritual side of youth. There are many wonderful programs with skilled professionals that don't attract youth because they are unable to produce the spark of fun, excitement and meaning that appeals to youth.

In later chapters, you will learn about the technical aspects of creating programs and activities — needs assessments, setting goals and objectives, program design and other topics.   First, however, it is important that you learn how to create magic for children in programs and activities . . . for without the magic, no amount of planning will compensate. Following are guidelines that create magic for youth!

Creating the Vision
- ❑ Knowing what you are trying to accomplish
- ❑ Visualizing the program or event
- ❑ Structuring the Sensory and Physical Environments
- ❑ Researching programs and events
- ❑ Using contemporary material
- ❑ Using principles of customer service

Creating the Environment
- ❑ Exceeding expectations
- ❑ Creating the illusion of a different time and place
- ❑ Adding the element of surprise/anticipation
- ❑ Creating perceived freedom/perceived competence
- ❑ Making the effort
- ❑ Attending to details that make a difference

Creating the Connection
- ❑ Making personal contact
- ❑ Being a kid
- ❑ Creating opportunities for social synergy

❑   Promoting ownership/empowerment
❑   Creating a core of meaningfulness

"Magic" moments in recreation programming are not an illusion or lucky accident, they can be systematically produced by following a prescribed course of action.

CREATING THE VISION

The most important factor in planning programs and events that achieve a high degree of excellence (and magic), is mentally visualizing the program. Before the youth leader engages in technical planning of programs and events, he/she needs to develop a mental picture or vision of what the program will be like.

Visualizing and researching programs or events, in terms of knowing what you want to accomplish, the needs and desires of youth that you are responding to, the effect you intend to create, use of contemporary material and engaging in customer service are all important in creating "magic" for youth.

❑   Knowing what you are trying to accomplish

❑   Visualizing the program or event

❑   Structuring the sensory and physical environments

❑   Researching programs and events

❑   Using contemporary material

❑   Using principles of customer service

Knowing What You are Trying to Accomplish

Many leaders believe that they are in the business of organizing activities, programs and events for youth. This is not the case. Rather, *the leader is in the business of creating an atmosphere or environment for youth that sets the stage for them to develop themselves,* including increasing their self-esteem, increasing their social skills, enhancing their physical development, exercising creativity, growing spiritually, learning cooperation, teamwork, leadership and other developmental knowledge and skills. In other words, youth leaders are involved in youth development.

In addition, the business of the youth leader is to create memorable, fulfilling moments for youth. The leader should understand the underlying purpose and outcomes of programs.

Visualizing the Program or Event

The leader engaged in planning should *mentally visualize any program, activity or event* from the time youth enter it until they leave. How will kids meet each other? Does it look like there will be periods of time where they will be just hanging around waiting? As you visualize going through the sequence of events, do you think you would enjoy them? What opportunities are available? What problems do you foresee? Is there a way that you can anticipate problems and deal with them ahead of time?

Structuring the Sensory and Physical Environments

Different types of lighting, colors, sound and spatial arrangements create different moods within recreation programs and activities. The leader can determine what type of environment he/she is trying to create and then *use light, sound, and spatial arrangements to create the magic.*

Does the leader want people to have a lot of room to move around, or does he/she want them clustered together to promote social interaction and a sense of closeness and togetherness? Loud rock music, bright lights and brightly colored "malt shop" decorations will create one type of mood, whereas James Bond music, a dimly lit room, and "international intrigue" decorations will create a different type of mood.

Researching Programs and Events

How do leaders come up with those wonderful, creative ideas that result in magic programs, activities and events? *The best leaders supplement their own creative ideas and energy with research.* Are you planning a program or event that focuses on the future? On space? On the environment? 50s theme? The effective youth leader will go to the library and check out books and other resources, or rent a relevant video, or ask someone who is knowledgeable in order to get input that supplements his/her ideas. Great ideas are usually a modification or adaptation of someone else's ideas.

Using Contemporary Material

No matter what activities and programs you are planning, they will be more successful if they relate to what youth are thinking about and what they are interested in. *Find out what is cool, hip, funky and "in."* Talk to your youth, and *listen* to them regarding what they are thinking and what they like, watch the shows geared for kids on TV, go to the latest kids' movies, watch the cartoons on Saturday mornings, find out what kids are studying in school. Take notes, and refer to them throughout the year. Focus your programming efforts on *what kids like, not what you think they will like.* Youth often have things done *to* them and *for* them, rather than with them and in "their world."

CREATING THE ENVIRONMENT

There are certain methods that the leader can use to develop program or activity environments that create "magic." The leader can create environments that exceed expectations and that offer a sense of illusion, a sense of being transported to another time and place, a sense of timelessness, and a sense of surprise and suspense.

❏   Exceeding expectations

❏   Creating the illusion of a different time and place

❏   Adding the element of surprise/anticipation

❏   Creating perceived freedom/perceived competence

❏   Making the effort

❏   Attending to details that make a difference

Exceeding Expectations

The single most important factor in creating magic moments for youth is to exceed their expectations. Did you ever go to a leisure activity as a child that exceeded your expectations to such a degree that it was a magic moment in your life? Youth should feel a sense of excitement and exhilaration because the activity is different, and BETTER than they ever thought it would be. They should say "I can't wait until the next time I come to the youth center to see what is going to happen next!"

Creating the Illusion of a Different Time and Place

The leader can create magic for youth by programming recreation activities and events that transcend time, place and space and *create an illusion that transports youth to a different dimension.* A facility can be decorated like a time tunnel, with a tunnel entrance that kids go through. Or it can represent the space world of Star Trek.

The Walt Disney corporation is familiar with the concept of creating and maintaining an illusion and uses it in their theme parks. Kids love it, and it can be applied within the youth center. To create an illusion of a different time and place during a theme week or theme month at the youth center, the leader should:

❏   **Dress the illusion.** Use some type of costume, make-up, hairdo, hat, or other elaborate or simple addition to your dress to be part of the illusion of the theme that you are creating. Also encourage kids to dress the illusion. If it is space week, have them make space antennae and wear them. If it is 50s week, show them the 50s look and encourage them to "grease out."

❑   **Talk the illusion.** The way that the leader talks and interacts with kids should support the illusion being created. If it is Star Trek week, instead of "don't run," tell kids not to go at "warp speed." Talk the language of the theme week/month.

❑   **Decorate the Illusion.** Decorations can be elaborate or simple, but they should support the illusion of the theme. Particularly effective is an entrance that kids can go through as they pass into the theme world, e.g. a tunnel, haunted house, magic jukebox.

❑   **Listen to the illusion.** The music at the center should support the illusion. If it is "Ultimate Undersea Adventure" week, play whale calls, music from The Little Mermaid, and other related music that supports the illusion.

❑   **Act out the illusion.** If it is 50s week, have kids make a soda shop, do Elvis air guitar, have a sock hop, learn rock and roll, make autograph books and otherwise act out the illusion.

❑   **Stay in character.** Stay in character with the theme. Of course you will talk to youth as you usually do, but also add in language and actions that support the theme throughout the theme week.

As indicated above, the youth leader can create the illusion of a different time and place by orchestrating, wall murals, music, costumes, decorations, adapting songs and games and using imaginative dialogue. This type of activity creates "magic" for youth.

What unusual decorations, or entrance can you create that will surprise youth, and exceed their expectations? For example, why not use an undersea theme, and have kids go through a "yellow submarine" on their way into the facility, with the song "Under the Sea" playing. These types of strategies, accompanied by other decorations, activities and arts and crafts will create a sense of excitement and anticipation.

Adding the Element of Surprise/Anticipation

An important part of creating magic is adding the element of surprise, as well as the element of anticipation. When the unexpected occurs, it contributes to the energy, excitement and fun of a program, activity or event. For example, a brief continuous activity that runs through your program or event can *add this element of the unexpected.*

Is your program or event related to space? Science? Rockets? Then have a "Mad Scientist" periodically run through the area in a white fright wig and lab coat, with a steaming beaker of colored "chemicals" enacting a funny skit with kids and leaders. This not only adds surprise, but kids anticipate his/her return, which maintains heightened interest and excitement. Maybe . . the mad scientist will even appear out on the soccer field, or. . . will be behind that tree, or . . .

Creating Perceived Freedom/
Perceived Competence

A critical element in creating magic, is allowing youth to experience perceived freedom and perceived competence. It has been found that when these two elements are present in a leisure activity, the participant experiences a state of "flow" — a feeling that time and place are suspended (Csikszentmihalyi, 1975).

"Perceived freedom" means that the leader creates opportunities for youth to choose from a variety of different activities, giving them the illusion (or reality) of *freedom of choice.* "Perceived competence" means that the leader designs programs so that youth are faced with *challenges that are at a level equal to their ability,* so that they can achieve success and feel "competent."

Making The Effort

Magic does not happen *"magically."* It can't be thrown together. The leader needs to believe in and enjoy programming for youth enough to commit the time and the physical and creative energy to create magic. *A high level of effort is required to do anything that is worthwhile and of quality.* The leader who throws together leisure activities for youth obtains results that are proportionate to the energy involved.

The best planning involves a group of people; a group endeavor will almost always surpass an individual one. First, it creates synergy between people — that is, they help each other come up with creative ideas that no one person could have thought of alone. Second, it creates energy, excitement and enthusiasm. And third, it is easier to delegate out a number of small tasks when more people are involved.

Attending to Details That Make the Difference

It is the details that often create the magic in recreation programming. When you program don't just do it so that it is "good enough." Do it so that it is the BEST that has ever been done by anyone anywhere. If you program in a way that exceeds your expectations and the expectations of the other staff, it will exceed the expectations of youth as well. Add the details in terms of costumes, prizes, decorations and attentiveness that tell youth you care about them — youth especially appreciate the things you didn't *have* to do. Those types of things make youth feel like you really care about them and that you value them. It is worth it to add the small details that create special, magic moments.

CREATING THE CONNECTION

What strategies can the leader use to connect with youth, and help them connect with each other within programs, activities and events? Even well-conceived programs, activities and events, will not reach their potential unless youth make meaningful contact with the leader and each other.

The leader needs to "be a kid" and be enthusiastically involved in the activity *with* youth. He or she should make personal contact with youth, create opportunities for social synergy, empower youth, draw youth into leadership of the activity and create a core of meaningfulness within the activity.

❑   Making personal contact

❑   Being a kid

❑   Creating opportunities for social synergy

❑   Promoting Ownership/Empowerment

❑   Creating a core of meaningfulness

Making Personal Contact

There is nothing worse than being part of a faceless, nameless crowd, with no real identity or sense of self. *The leader should make a point of treating each youth as an individual.* Make eye contact, call youth by name, give them a pat on the back, ask them questions about themselves.

If the number of youth is too large to make individual contact, then do it symbolically. Bring some of the youth to the front of the group and interact with them individually and humorously, and the crowd will feel a sense of personal recognition indirectly. Have you seen an entertainer work a crowd to create magic that relates to each individual?

Being a Kid

To create magic, the leader can't simply do things *to* and *for* youth, but needs to be involved *with* youth. *A leader who directs the activity as a separate uninvolved adult entity destroys the illusion of the program, activity or event.* In order to be effective, the leader needs to be able to be spontaneous, fun-loving, and involved *with* youth in the activities. It is hard for anyone to have fun and let go, when being watched from the sidelines by people who are above participating.

Promoting Ownership/Empowerment

A goal of the leader should always be to encourage owner-ship, empowerment and leadership of youth in leisure pro-grams, activities and events. Rather than have the staff plan for youth, the leader should *draw in youth to help in the planning and execution of programs,* activities and events. Youth can give valuable input regarding what kids like and want, and they can provide manpower that enables the leader to provide larger more complex programs and events. Also, kids will have more fun and will be more involved when they or their friends are involved in leading the programs and activities.

Creating Opportunities for Social Interaction

A key element in creating "magic" is creating opportunities for youth to interact with one another in a positive, creative manner. The leader should not assume that youth will get to know each other on their own. The leader should build within programs and activities catalysts that *promote interaction between youth.* Particularly, when the leader is working with a large group, it should be broken down into smaller, more intimate, groups if possible so that kids can interact more easily.

To promote interaction, the leader can have kids: 1) wear something special to activities (beach clothes, space antennae, backward clothes); 2) group youth together to do skit in a bag; 3) have youth help lead activities, songs, games; 4) group youth into special interest clubs of their choice. Also, the leader should be sure that activities, programs and events are structured so that *everyone* can participate.

Creating a Core of Meaningfulness

Have you ever attended a recreation activity in which you had fun, but you left feeling that it had been a waste of your time? For both kids and adults, *meaningfulness is an important part of leisure activities.* Meaningfulness in activities may be concrete, like incorporating environmental concepts into a field trip, or it may be less tangible like spiritual closeness that can occur with other people singing quiet songs in a group.

People have a natural desire to learn, develop, connect, grow, achieve and excel. The leader should be aware of this fact, and help to create a core of meaningfulness in programs and activities. Having traditions within your programs, having quiet, close group times of sharing, giving youth an opportunity to plan and lead activities, offering them opportunities to learn, allowing them opportunities to help others, all contribute to a sense of meaningfulness.

A Final Note

Magic moments don't occur "magically" — they don't just happen. They require planning, effort and commitment. Is it worth it to spend hours, days, weeks, maybe months planning programs, activities and events that are often over in a short period of time, maybe an hour or two? Yes, because magic moments of childhood last a lifetime. They shape who we are, how we feel about ourselves and our feelings of self-confidence and competence.

Not only do such activities help youth develop socially, emotionally, physically and spiritually, but they create memories that will bring lasting pleasure and personal enrichment. The leader engaged in leisure programming is engaged in a most worthwhile endeavor.

Personal Notes:
Creating Magic

Now that you have an understanding of how to create "magic" for youth, create a "magic moment" by using the guidelines that have been discussed. Mentally visualize a program that you could carry out at your youth center.

❑   **Mentally visualize the program you want to offer:**

_____

_____

Now that you have visualized it, before you carry it out find out if kids want it, need it, or have other ideas.

❑   Tell how your program will exceed kids' expectations, and add the element of surprise. How will you promote interaction between kids?

_____

The element of surprise not only is fun, in itself, for kids, but it then creates the excitement of anticipation — whether another surprise will happen again.

❑   Will you create an illusion of a different time and place and if so how?

_____

The entrance to the center, decorations, music, spatial arrangements, lighting, refreshments, costumes, and dialogue can create this effect.

❑   What activities will you offer to create perceived freedom and perceived competence? Will you offer opportunities for youth input and leadership?

_____

Offering several activities and then letting youth choose gives them a feeling of freedom and independence. They must be able to successfully accomplish activities, but not too easily, to feel competent.

❑   A core of meaningfulness is crucial. How can you help kids feel that their program experience is meaningful?

_____

Quiet songs, learning, sharing, leading, helping others add meaning to programs.

References

Csikszentmihalyi, M. (1975). *Beyond Boredom and Anxiety*. San Francisco: Jossey-Bass.

Edginton, C. R. and S. R. Edginton. (Winter, 1992). Creating Magic the *Camp Adventure*™ Way. *Humanics: The Journal of Leadership for Youth and Human Service.*,Winter, p.4-7.

Edginton, S. (1993). Camp Adventure: A New, Innovative Youth Services Practicum Opportunity. *Renaissance Group Newsletter,* 1(2), pp. 9.

Edginton, C. and L.J. Luneckas. (1993). Creating Magic at *Camp Adventure*™. *Parks & Recreation,* 27(11), pp 68-73.

CHAPTER 3

CUSTOMER SERVICE

Youth, as well as parents and others in the community, are all customers. It is the responsibility of the leader to make youth feel valued, appreciated, and to provide programs and services that appropriately reward and respect their investment of time and energy. Listening, being responsive to needs and concerns, being caring, providing a clean and safe environment, enhancing experiences, and adding value to services are all ways that the youth leader can use principles of customer service to serve youth, as well as others in the community.

Customer service principles are the focus of this chapter. Customer service helps the youth leader connect with youth, parents, and the community to provide programs that achieve a high level of excellence. In this chapter, we will review the elements of customer service excellence and how to gain and use input from customers to improve services. We will discuss some of the activities consistent with good customer service, including exceeding expectations, anticipating needs, seeking to improve services, and effective handling of complaints.

As a result of participation in this chapter of the book you will be able to:

▶ Make customers feel that you and your organization value them.

▶ Exhibit greater sensitivity to issues related to the needs of customers.

▶ Increase the effectiveness of your organization in handling complaints.

CUSTOMER SERVICE

The phrase "customer service" refers to the way in which the youth leader responds to the needs of customers (youth/parents/ community) in order to provide the best possible service and, as a result, customer satisfaction. How does the youth leader know what constitutes good customer service? This section will review the *elements of customer service excellence and how to gain and use input from customers to improve services.* Some of the activities consistent with good customer service as adapted from Edginton, Hanson and Edginton (1992) are:

❑   Exceeding expectations

❑   Anticipating needs

❑   Solving problems

❑   Caring about customers

❑   Being knowledgeable/competent

❑   Seeking to improve services

❑   Consistency and reliability

❑   Showing respect for customers

❑   Maintaining the work environment

❑   Appropriate dress/demeanor

❑   Knowing what business you are in

Organizations that are sincerely interested in creating and maintaining the highest level of customer service train and empower their youth leaders to meet customer needs as they judge appropriate. The effective youth leader places a high priority on "customer service."

Customer service helps the youth leader connect with customers (including youth, parents, and the community) to provide programs and services that achieve a high level of excellence, result in increased participation and that enhance the image of the organization.

Exceeding Expectations

Providing services that *exceed what customers have asked for* or have paid for is the goal of the leader. If the leader does not accomplish this goal (exceed expectations), customers will view the program or service only as adequate or less than adequate. This is especially challenging, since each customer will come to the organization with *different* expectations.

The youth leader should attempt to view programs, activities and events from the point of view of youth and their parents. If you were the participant, would your expectations be exceeded by the service your organization is providing? Or would you view the service as mediocre?

Anticipating Needs

Assessing and *anticipating customer needs and ensuring that the programs and services offered by the organization are consistent with customer needs*, is an important function of the leader. It is not sufficient for the leader to simply *meet* a customer's needs; the effective leader should *anticipate* needs before the customer may even be aware of them, and plan accordingly. For example, if a child forgets lunch money for a field trip, has the leader anticipated the contingency and brought extra money or an extra lunch?

Solving Problems

A problem-solving customer service orientation places the needs of the customer first. In effect, the leader/customer relationship is based on the welfare of the customer and resolving problems that stand in the way of total customer satisfaction. The organization should attempt to provide support to customers by *building into its programs and services components that will assist them in solving problems.* For example, adding latch key programs before and after summer day camp programs is a customer service factor that is supportive to working parents. What other problems can your organization solve?

Caring About Customers (Youth/Parents/Community)

An organization that cares about its customers will engender loyalty and support. *Leaders should demonstrate genuine and sincere caring* for youths and parents. The needs of the customer should take priority over the problems of staff; the customer comes first.

The leader should work to *make customers knowledgeable about the organization and its programs and activities.* All great leaders are teachers. Parents have natural concerns regarding the safety and quality of services, the experience of staff, and other concerns. Youth have anxieties about their success in new activities, their entry into the group and their interaction with the leader. The leader can recognize this and work to alleviate concerns.

Being Knowledgeable/Competent

Effective leaders should *possess appropriate knowledge* to provide services of high caliber. A youth leader needs to have well-developed knowledge, skills and abilities in order to successfully provide services to youths and parents that meet standards for excellence. Leaders should be knowledgeable about the overall and specific organizational goals that relate to the customer service mission.

Remember that *the youth leader is not only interacting with the customer,* but is indirectly interacting with the customer's family, friends, supervisor, and others. Youths and parents will talk either positively or negatively about your organization and its services to others.

Seeking to Improve Services

As leaders plan and implement programs and activities, they should look for ways to improve their services, based upon both personal observations and input from supervisors, youths and parents. Are you open to input and suggestions? Do you look for ways to innovate?

Effective leaders *listen carefully to customers.* The more we know about individuals, the better we are able to help them. What are the things that customers say they would like to do? What do they like or not like about services? The leisure field is rapidly changing, with new fads on the horizon every few months. Listen to young people, so that your programs and activities have appeal for today's kids.

Maintaining Consistency and Reliability

The challenge to the youth leader is not only to provide services of the highest level of excellence, but to do so reliably and consistently. Youth and other customers should be able *to depend on the quality of services and find the same high quality programs, activities and events every time* that they choose to participate.

Showing Respect for Customers

Successful leaders show respect for customers. *Treat customers (youth, parents) as if they were guests in your own home.* Don't focus on the organization and its concerns, focus on your customer. Allow customers the power to make choices. Rather than having things planned and organized in a linear fashion, offer customers (youth) several options, so that they have the feeling that they have had input into their choices and experiences.

Maintaining the Work Environment

Customers develop an opinion of an organization based upon not only their interactions with youth leaders and supervisory staff, but by their perception of the orderliness of the work environment. *Customers form an opinion of your organization based upon what they see;* they can't know what goes on behind the scenes.

If they see an organized, orderly youth center that appears to be well-maintained and clean, they will conclude that your organization is also well-organized. Conversely, if the center is cluttered, dirty, with sloppy bulletin boards, they will conclude that your organization is unorganized.

Appropriate Dress/Demeanor

The *dress and demeanor of the youth leader and other staff will influence customers' perceptions of the organization.* If staff are dressed professionally and neatly, the effect upon customers will be different than if staff are in jeans and t-shirts and don't look "together."

Even part-time staff, volunteers, interns and student help should be counseled regarding their dress and personal demeanor, because the customer may not know the difference between these employees and permanent staff.

Knowing What Business You Are In

Leaders in the leisure service field are *not* in the business of providing programs and activities, they are in *the business of providing happiness, personal growth and development, self-esteem and belonging.* These activities should be the focus of your efforts.

A Final Note

Youth services organizations that are dedicated to promoting satisfaction among customers will increase their likelihood of short- and long-term success. Positive customer relations are primarily dependent upon front-line staff members. It is the front line staff of a youth services organization that is its first point of contact with youth. The front line of any organization is its "bottom line."

An Emphasis on Customer Service Builds Customer Satisfaction and Loyalty

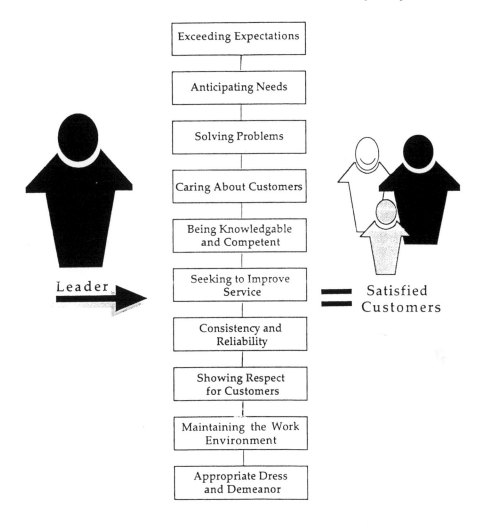

Personal Notes:
Customer Service

Customer service does not necessarily need to be based on a set of rules that you must remember. Customer service is no more than treating your customers at work (youth, parents, community) the same way that you would *treat guests in your own home.*

If you have guests come to your home, what are some of the things you would do?

_____

_____

_____

_____

_____

_____

_____

You would be glad to see them, greet them by name, smile, make eye contact, take their coat, reminisce about past meetings, offer them something to eat/drink, offer to take them places to have new experiences and you would have cleaned your home and dressed neatly prior to their arrival. When they left, you would thank them for coming, compliment them on the nice visit and ask them to come again. Possibly you would give them information about plans for their next future visit. All of these actions will make your customers at work feel valued as well.

References

Edginton, C.R. , C. J. Hansen and S. R. Edginton. (1992). *Leisure Programming: Concepts, Trends and Professional Practice.* Dubuque, IA: Brown and Benchmark.

CHAPTER 4

TQP LEADER CHECKLIST

Effective leadership is a key element in planning, organizing, and implementing youth programs and services. The provision of quality services often revolves around creating positive youth leader/customer interactions. The successful youth leader is one who is aware of the way in which his/her actions impact upon youth.

Practical experience in the youth services area results in the discovery of leadership techniques that are successful in interacting positively with youth. The checklist in this chapter offers an overview of "youth leadership tips" that have been shown to be effective in increasing the level of excellence and effectiveness of programs and activities.

As a result of reviewing this chapter, you will be able to:

▶ Plan and program activities and programs with a greater degree of effectiveness and excellence.

▶ Exhibit greater sensitivity to issues related to youth development, youth involvement, behavior management and others.

▶ Increase the impact of programming by planning opportunities for youth for involvement, leadership and recognition.

TOTAL QUALITY PROGRAM PLANNING: LEADER CHECKLIST

The youth leader committed to Total Quality Program Planning (TQP) creates services that are developmentally sound, caring, effective, meaningful and fun. TQP programs exceed the expectations of youth, their parents and the community.

This chapter presents a checklist of tips for the youth leader to assist in the planning and implementation of programs. Many of these tips are discussed in greater detail in other chapters of the book.

✔ *Build in opportunities for youth leadership and involvement . . .*

❐ Encourage youth leadership. Let youth plan and carry out some activities. Develop and/or use youth advisory groups and councils and rotate group leadership among different children.

❐ Give youth a sense of freedom of choice. If you give them several choices of what to do, and let them pick one, they feel that they have input and ownership.

❐ Go with the flow when implementing programs, try to be flexible. Let youth have some influence over the way in which activities and programs unfold.

❐ Help kids learn strategies and activities that will allow them to be independent and self-directed. Have available programs and activities that youth can initiate themselves.

❐ In groups that have a wide range of ages, encourage the older children to help plan and implement activities for younger children; give them opportunities for leadership and responsibility.

✔ *Invest the time it takes to provide great programs . . .*

☐   Find out what youth really want to do; don't just program according to what *you think they want to do*. Have youth provide information about their wants and needs, through youth councils, youth advisory groups, needs assessments, surveys or by just talking to them.

☐   Staff should be extremely well-organized, have a high degree of structure for what will take place, yet allow the children freedom within structure.

☐   Make sure that all the children have something to do within activities. If you offer a cooking activity, rather than having one person stir the mixture, with 15 people watching, have the other people coloring pictures of cookies, or some other activity.

☐   Play "with" the kids; be willing to be a kid again yourself. If you participate and have fun, kids will too. If the activities are too childish for you and you stand on the sidelines kids will also be reluctant to participate. They will follow your lead.

☐   Add the element of excitement, surprise and anticipation to your programs. Kids should say to themselves "I can't wait to get to the youth center to see what will happen next."

☐   Plan ahead. Quality programs require quality effort. Kids will get out of activities and programs as much as you are willing to put into them. Allow at least 30 days to plan larger activities.

☐   Anticipate — think about what might go wrong, and have a "Plan B" in place to take care of potential problems.

❏   When children are present, they are your number one priority. Stay out with the kids, rather than in the office. Staff should be interacting with the children, not grouped on the sidelines.

❏   Activities that require a lot of effort on the part of staff, communicate to kids that you must care a lot about them to put in the time and effort for them.

✔ *Be sure that programs support youth development . . .*

❏   Try to say "yes" to youth. If they have ideas, be the person that helps them remove barriers so that their ideas can happen. If it can't be done, guide them in a positive way in another direction.

❏   Make sure that activities provided for youth are age-appropriate. That is, they should be geared to the developmental stages of the different age groups. If activities are too easy, youth will get bored; if they are too hard, they will get frustrated.

❏   If you have a range of ages of children, segment them into age groups for activities, or if this is not possible, modify activities for the various age groups.

❏   Integrate youth development competencies into your programs and activities, including health/physical competencies, personal/social, cognitive/creative, vocational and citizenship.

❏   As you assume a leadership role, be a positive role model for the children you serve. They will watch you, act like you, talk like you and assume many of your values. Since you will transmit values to the children; have you thought about which values you believe to be important?

❏　Decide in advance what the goals of your program will be. Will it be developmental? In what way? Is it instructional? Is it social? What do you want the children to be able to do or demonstrate after participating in your program?

❏　Choose each day a balance of activities from the four activity groups of — physical/sports, arts/crafts/drama, science/nature, and values/citizenship/vocation.

❏　*Every* child has the potential to be athletic, artistic, and creative in some way. It is up to the youth leader to bring these skills out.

❏　Find out about youth development and the needs of youth, as well as what children should learn and experience to become positive, productive adults.

✔　*Practice good customer service . . .*

❏　Youth are your customers, you have been hired to help serve their needs. One of the most important things you will do in your life is to create positive moments for these children that they will remember the rest of their lives.

❏　Handle any staff disagreements out of the range of hearing of children or other customers. Staff should treat each other professionally and with respect at all times, in order to maintain the respect of children and customers.

❏　The way you answer phones, talk to parents and talk to other staff reflects on your organization. Even personal conversations at work are observed by children, parents and others.

❒   Dress appropriately, professionally and neatly. Show that you care about yourself and the job that you do.

❒   Handle complaints promptly. If you do, research shows that the person complaining will tell others about how well the complaint was handled, offsetting the damage of the problem.

❒   Keep in mind that you are at all times a representative of your organization, even after work. Individuals who work with children must maintain a professional image at all times.

❒   Be a "can do" person, not a barrier person with youth, your boss, parents. When you are asked to do something, think about how you can work around the barriers, rather than dwelling on all the reasons why you "can't do it."

❒   It is your personal responsibility to look over your facility and the grounds around it daily, to be sure that they are safe for the children. If you see any safety hazards, take care of them immediately; don't wait for someone else to do it. Then follow-up to be sure it has been done.

❒   Your facility and grounds should be clean and well-organized at all times. If people see a messy facility, they assume that the organization is disorganized.

✔ *Use positive behavior management . . .*

❒   Speak to children positively. *Never* yell at a child; *never* touch a child in anger. Never means never.

❒   Speak to children in a normal, positive, firm voice and they will respond to you. If you speak normally they will be quiet to hear you; yell and they will tune you out. Use behavior management strategies, such as "Clap once if you can hear me. Now clap twice if you can hear me" until all of the children are clapping and quiet.

☐ Believe in what you are doing. Interact with children energetically and positively; expect kids to want to participate and have fun. If you seem uncertain, they will pick up on it. "People won't follow an uncertain trumpet."

☐ Kids are just like you — they want to be helpful, to learn new things, to do things that are worthwhile for others, and to have fun. It is your job to help them over negative barriers so that they can behave in the way that is most natural to them.

☐ Kids that "act out" in negative ways don't feel part of the group. Use strategies to help them feel more a part of the group.

☐ If children are asked to be quiet when staff are talking to them, you should also set an example and be quiet and attentive when your other staff members are talking.

☐ Use reinforcement techniques daily and weekly to help kids modify their behavior in a positive way. Change the methods you use frequently, before they lose their influence.

☐ Always focus on the positive. Rather than focus on the one child that is not quiet in the group, focus on the child who is quiet. Say " Wow. . . Joshua is listening!" If a child continues to disrupt the group, remove him/her from the group and talk to him/her separately; don't allow him/her to get negative attention.

☐ It is important for all staff to decide together what the rules will be for the children, and then support each other in reinforcing them. One staff person should not have one set of rules, and another staff member another set of rules.

❏ You will get what you expect. If you expect children to be bright, attentive, capable, helpful and to exhibit behavior that is respectful of you and other children, you will get it. If children have not learned how to behave in an acceptable manner, you will need to use the techniques in this book to help them "practice" to achieve acceptable behavior. Also reward them for positive behavior.

❏ Make sure that each child hears more positive things from you than negative ones. If you have not said at least two positive things to a child during the day, do not criticize the child, unless safety is a factor. Wait until the child has heard a few good things from you first, so that there will be an appropriate sense of balance; the child knows that his/her behavior is mostly "good" and correct.

✔ *And, last, but most importantly . . .*

❏ Remember the most important part of being a youth leader . . .

HAVE FUN!

PART II

YOUTH DEVELOPMENT

CHAPTER 5

TRENDS AND ISSUES
RELATED TO YOUTH

The goal of youth leaders, family members, and communities is to nurture children and youth in a manner that allows them to develop into positive adult members of society. Today, youth are being challenged by societal forces that have the potential to dramatically impact them. Lack of opportunity, substance abuse, change in family dynamics and other factors place a large number of youth at risk. Knowledge of trends and issues affecting youth can help youth leaders and organizations respond accordingly, in a proactive manner.

This chapter offers information for the youth leader about trends and issues that may have an impact on youth. In order to plan effectively for youth, the leader must have knowledge about current trends and their potential impact on youth, as well as issues that may suggest a need for certain types of youth programming.

As a result of participation in this section you will be able to:

▶ Understand some of the social trends that relate to youth.

▶ Gain knowledge about how youth spend their time.

▶ Increase the impact of programming by responding to current issues and trends that may have an impact on youth.

YOUTH TRENDS AND ISSUES

This chapter will present information about trends impacting on youth and some of the issues that will have an impact on your efforts to provide quality services for youth. A model that shows the "big picture" of some of the issues, values and developmental objectives that are involved in youth development within recreation programs is presented in this section. As the model shows, there will be an interaction between various issues, such as community needs, family structure and social trends and our values that relate to youth.

Some issues related to youth will impact on our values. As issues and values interact, they contribute to the formation of developmental objectives and to a commitment to include developmental objectives in programs.

The following will give you an example of how to interpret this chart:

❑   Family structure and roles is a current social issue. There are more single parents and mothers who work.

❑   This issue may impact on, or suggest, values related to community involvement, family involvement, self-reliance and self-esteem.

❑   To respond to these issues and values, the youth leader may incorporate into programs developmental objectives related to personal/social competence to help youth develop friendships and relationships, coping skills, judgement skills (decision-making/problem-solving), and life skills

These types of skills may help youth to be more resilient in the face of the challenges and changes related to today's evolving family structures.

ISSUES THAT AFFECT YOUTH

As a youth leader, there are a number of issues that you will need to consider in planning and programming for youth. Issues such as increasing diversity, fewer resources, and a changing family structure, may influence the demand for certain types of programs and services. These issues will suggest program needs and/or leadership considerations. Following are some of these issues:

❑ **Treating Youth as "Whole" Individuals.** An important issue is the need to treat youth as "whole" individuals. Youth are often treated as if they are made up of segments or parts — the school deals with one part, the family deals with another part, a youth leader may deal with another area. The committed youth leader will design programs that accomplish the goal of producing a "whole" physically healthy, mentally healthy and intellectually-challenged youth.

The leader may need to coordinate with other agencies and individuals who serve youth so that the needs of the whole *young individual* are met. Several new model programs are being developed that offer youth a number of opportunities in after-school recreation programs, including *leisure programs, health counseling, psychological counseling and tutoring for school.*

❑ **Greater Diversity.** The U.S. population will become more diverse within the next decade. This is an issue that will impact organizations, and will have implications for program planning.

❑ **Fewer Resources.** There are fewer resources today. As a youth leader you may need to be entrepreneurial (expanding program opportunities for youth through creative means, such as cooperative efforts with other organizations/clubs, fund-raising events, or other strategies).

YOUTH DEVELOPMENT

YOUTH DEVELOPMENT
YOUTH DEVELOPMENT
YOUTH DEVELOPMENT

ISSUES	↔	VALUES	→	DEVELOPMENT OBJECTIVES

ISSUES	VALUES	DEVELOPMENT OBJECTIVES
• Family Structure/Patterns	• Self-Reliance	• Personal Development
• Decline in Social Health	• Respect for Others	• Social Development
• Decline in Physical Health	• Citizenship	• Emotional Development
• Greater Diversity	• Independence and Responsibility	• Physiological Development
• Greater Mobility		• Intellectual Development
• Changing Community Needs	• Lifelong Leisure	• Life Skills
• Fewer Resources	• Compassion and Commitment	
• Need to View "Whole" Youth	• Individuality/ Peer Pressure	
• Increase in Substance Abuse	• Leadership	
• Increase in Physical/ Emotional Abuse	• Trust	
• Youth Involvement/ Leadership	• Teamwork/ Competitiveness	
	• Quality/Excellence	
	• Loyalty	
	• Integrity	
	• Family Unity	

❏   **Changing Family Structure.** Youth leaders will need to respond to issues related to changing family structures. More working mothers, single parent families, blended families (children from two former families) impact on the types of support and services that will meet youths' needs.

❏   **Increased Violence Toward Children and Youth.** One of the most important issues that you must be aware of as a youth leader, is the increase of violence toward children and youth. Your community has in place procedures for dealing with youth who have been abused. Make sure you are familiar with this process.

❏   **Changing Community Needs.** The needs of your community are constantly changing. Latchkey programs, fitness programs, outreach programs have all been developed to meet changing needs. You will need to keep "tuned in" to the needs of youth and parents within your community in order to respond to new needs as they are identified.

❏   **Physical Decline of Youth.** On a national basis, youth have been found to be in a state of physical decline. Youth leaders will want to respond to this issue by providing opportunities for physical activities and fitness programs.

❏   **Greater Mobility.** Youth are more mobile today and as a result have special needs in this area. As a youth leader, you should have in place programs and activities that support youth who are in transition.

These and other social trends have the potential to impact upon youth and, as such, should be considered by the youth leader when engaged in program planning.

Issues Related to Program Participation

Other issues have been brought up that compare activity patterns among youth with program needs. There are some important issues that *youth leaders must address if they wish to increase participation levels* among youth. Following are five (5) such issues as adapted from Kwak (1992).

❑   Young adolescents do not spend large amounts of time engaged in activities sponsored by public . . . agencies, but *the things they do are valued.*

❑   The public . . . sector tends to concentrate its efforts on providing for those inclined to participate. *The needs or interests of non-users are rarely considered.*

❑   Service providers are not always anxious or willing to plan programs around the *expressed preference or interests of young adolescents.*

❑   Young *adolescents of different backgrounds share some interests in common, but they also differ in many ways.* If public . . . providers wish to increase participation in their programs, they must design services targeted at specific populations and improve their marketing skills.

❑   There must be a careful *balance between providing structured programs and providing safe* . . . *[local]* . . . *facilities* where young adolescents can be together on their own terms.

Regarding the last participation issue above, it is important to keep in mind that youth have their lives programmed and scheduled from early morning and through the day. They have school lessons, clubs, church activities and other planned and structured activities. The leader will want to create an environment within youth programs and activities in which there are opportunities for youth to engage in self-direction and self-development.

CURRENT SOCIAL TRENDS

There are a number of national social trends that may impact upon youth today. Why does the youth leader, need to be aware of these trends? Knowledge of these trends will help you understand why the types of services you provide are so important for youth. These trends may also suggest to you ideas for programs that would help meet the needs of youth.

The information presented regarding trends related to youth, adapted from Scales (1991), is varied in terms of age groupings. For example, some studies discuss youth 6-12, others discuss youth 10-15, and so on. However, the information forms a broad picture that can help the leader provide better programming based on an understanding of youth and their needs.

- **Diversity.** The proportion of non-white youth is projected to increase dramatically by the year 2000. *By the year 2000, the U.S. Census predicts that 34% of the nation's children will be African American, Latino and Asian.*

  Do you have a plan for programs and activities that celebrate different ethnic and cultural groups? Are you aware of techniques you can use to reduce prejudice and build self-esteem?

- **Physical Health.** A 1990 national commission report stated that "for the first time in the history of this country, young people are less healthy and less prepared to take their places in society than were their parents." (National Commission on the Role of the School and the Community in Improving Adolescent Health, 1990.)

  Do you have fitness activities and programs available to youth? Do you consider physical health and development when you plan your youth programs?

■   **Social Health.** Social health includes such factors as success in school, being substance-free, and other behaviors in accordance with social mores, or what is considered "normal" in society.

According to a study by the Fordham Institute, the social health of youth in the United States dropped almost 50% within the last 20 years (Jennings, 1989).

Research for the Carnegie Commission states that approximately one half of youth 10-17 are at risk for failing at school, drug abuse, becoming an adolescent parent, or delinquent behavior (Ooms and Herendeen, 1989).

As a youth leader, do you have in place activities and programs that offer relevant information and foster a sense of purpose, meaningfulness and belonging, to counteract the growing problems associated with the decline in the "social health" of youth?

■   **Physical/Emotional Abuse.** Depending on the definition of abuse used in reporting incidents, the following are reported.

Mistreatment of children increased between 60% and 150% during the 1990s.

Youth ages 12-14 were found to be abused at a higher rate than any other age group according to the U.S. Department of Health and Human Service.

The youth leader has a responsibility to be aware of and to be responsive to the increased incidence of child abuse. There has been a dramatic increase in the mistreatment of youth in the last decade.

■   **Family Structure/Patterns**

Family structure and family patterns have changed greatly in the last two decades.

It is predicted that nearly all children in the 6-12 year-old age group will need out-of-school-care by 1995 (Scales, 1991).

Youth will have an increasing need for community youth services and other youth programs outside of school. Youth today are more likely to live in families with a mother that works outside the home, in single-parent families, in blended families and in smaller families.

A Final Note

Current and future trends related to the physical and social health of youth, diversity, family structure and patterns and other factors have implications for program planning. The youth leader familiar with youth issues and trends will be able to plan and offer programs that anticipate and meet the needs of youth in an effective manner.

Personal Notes:
Trends and Issues

What activities or programs might you offer that would celebrate diversity? Build self-esteem?

_____

_____

_____

_____

What activities or programs might you offer to counteract the physical decline of youth?

_____

_____

_____

_____

What types of programs might you offer to respond to the fact that many youth come from families in which both parents work, and, as a result, they must be able to operate more independently and make responsible choices?

_____

_____

_____

_____

What types of programs might you offer to respond to the decline in social health of youth—in order to build youths' self-esteem and give them a sense of belonging?

_____

_____

_____

_____

References

Jennings, L. (1989). Fordham Institute's Index Documents Steep Decline in Children's and Youth's Social Health Since 1970. *Education Week. 9*, (9).

Kwak, C. (1992). *Adolescent Time Use and Its Implications for Youth Serving Agencies.* St. Paul, MN: National Youth Leadership Council.

National Commission on the Role of the School and the Community in Improving Adolescent Health. (1990).*Code Blue: Uniting for Healthier Youth.* Alexandria, VA: National Association of State Boards of Education.

Ooms,T. and L. Herendeen (1989). *Adolescent Substance Abuse Treatment: Evolving Policy at Federal, State and City Levels.* Washington, D.C.: Family Impact Seminar, American Association for Marriage and Family Therapy.

Scales, P. (1991). *A Portrait of Youth Adolescents in the 1990s.* Carborro, NC: Center for Early Adolescence.

CHAPTER 6

LIFE AGES/
STAGES OF YOUTH

Promoting the healthy growth of youth as they develop within the context of family, school, and community, is an important function of the youth leader. Leaders who base programs and activities on a foundation of youth development will increase the likelihood of positive outcomes for youth they serve.

This chapter offers information about the developmental characteristics of different age groups, or "stage" groups, of youth; that is, youth in various stages of development. In order to plan effectively for youth, the leader must have knowledge regarding developmental characteristics.

As a result of reading this chapter you will be able to:

▶ Program more effectively, basing programming on knowledge of the developmental characteristics of youth.

▶ Offer youth programs that are at their developmental level and so challenge them, but do not frustrate them.

▶ Increase the impact of programming by responding to both "age appropriateness" and "individual appropriateness."

LIFE AGES/ STAGES OF YOUTH

Magic moments for children and youth often occur in programs that offer them an opportunity to *grow and develop* as individuals. As a youth leader, you will have an opportunity to plan programs and activities that give youth positive support, as well as help them grow and develop in a number of ways. Understanding of the qualities that characterize youth of different ages is important if the youth leader is to plan effectively and to meet youths' needs.

This chapter of the book will offer information to help the youth leader understand how youth develop in terms of four aspects of their growth, including the following:

❑   Personality Development

❑   Cognitive Development

❑   Physical Development

❑   Affective Development

As youth grow, they strive to meet their basic physical, psychological and social needs and to build their knowledge, values and skills.   Each age has distinct characteristic abilities, attitudes and focuses, that are different from other stages of development. The descriptions provided for these age categories should serve as a guideline; all youth will not fall within these categories.

In this chapter, the youth leader will gain information about the two categories of personality development that occur during school-age (the ages of youth for which the leader will program). In addition, the leader will gain general information regarding other areas of development, as well as guidelines for programming for specific age categories.

PERSONALITY DEVELOPMENT

One concept of youth development has been developed by psychologist Erik Erikson (1963). He indicates that youth (as well as adults) progress through eight life stages related to personality development and that within each stage they establish new orientations to themselves and other people in their social world. At each life stage youth need to master a new level of social interaction, and as this process takes place their personality can be changed either positively or negatively.

At each stage, youth must resolve particular psychosocial crises, or challenges, in order to move to the next stage of personality development. Erikson says that youth need to achieve competency, a personal identity, and a feeling of closeness or intimacy with others within this process. As youth move through these life stages, they ask and answer such questions as "Am I normal?" "Am I lovable?" "Am I competent?" "Am I loving to others?" As the youth leader works with young people it is important to help them answer these questions "yes!"

Following is a brief description of Erikson's life stages as adapted from his book *Childhood and Society* (Erikson, 1963).

> **Trust vs. Mistrust (first year of life):** Depending on the quality of care received, the infant learns to trust the environment, to perceive it as orderly and predictable, or to be suspicious, fearful and mistrusting.
>
> **Autonomy vs. Doubt (second and third years of life):** The development of motor and mental abilities and the opportunity to explore, encourage a sense of autonomy and independence. However, if the child is excessively criticized or limited in his/her exploration, it will lead to a sense of doubt over his/her adequacy and competency.
>
> **Initiative vs. Guilt (fourth to fifth year of life):** The way adults respond to the child's self-initiated activities creates either a sense of freedom and initiative, or a sense of being an inept intruder in an adult world.
>
> **Industry vs. Inferiority (sixth to eleventh year):** The child has a concern for how things work and how they ought to operate, leading to a sense of industry in forming rules, organizing, ordering. However, if these efforts are rebuffed as silly, it may lead to a sense of inferiority. During this stage of development, outside influences

During this stage of development, outside influences begin to exert a greater influence on the child's development.

Identity vs. Role Confusion (twelve to eighteen years): The adolescent begins to develop the ability to see things from others' point of view. The youth must develop a sense of his or her own identity, as distinct from all others and personally acceptable, or he/she will be confused or settle on a "negative" identity, such as "class clown" or "speed freak."

Intimacy vs. Isolation (young adulthood): The consequences of the young adults' attempts at reaching out to make contact with others may result in a commitment to other persons or isolation from close personal relationships.

Generativity vs. Self-Absorption (middle age): At this stage, one may become concerned about their family, society and future generations, or may become concerned with only material possessions and physical well-being.

Integrity vs. Despair (old age): One looks back at life with a sense of fulfillment and integrity, or despair, feeling that life has been misdirected.

What does a review of these life stages mean to the youth leader? Why is it important to have this type of information? Having knowledge of these life stages helps to give the youth leader a more complete picture of youth and the challenges they must face and overcome, in order to mature into healthy, positive, productive adults.

DEVELOPMENTALLY-
APPROPRIATE PROGRAMMING

When the youth leader selects and carries out programs, it is important to choose activities that match the level of development of youth. Why is this important? It is important because if the leader chooses activities that are too difficult, then children will become frustrated. On the other hand, if the leader chooses activities that are too easy, children will not be challenged and will lose interest.

This chapter offers a set of guidelines for youth leaders so that they may provide developmentally-appropriate programming. Seven principles of developmentally-appropriate programming, as adapted from Albrecht and Plantz (1991), are discussed, as well as charts for each age grouping with information to assist the leader in planning programs and activities.

Seven Rules for Developmentally-
Appropriate Programming

Following are seven fundamental principles of developmentally-appropriate programming for school-age children:

1. Developmentally-appropriate programs are *tailored to the developmental characteristics and needs of the children and youth they serve.* Programs approach these developmental realities as opportunities, rather than problems.

2. Developmentally-appropriate school-age programs *provide resourceful, caring staff* who understand the changing roles adults play in youths' lives.

3. In developmentally-appropriate school-age programs, *both mixed-age grouping and same-age grouping are used to facilitate the development* of peer relations and social skills.

4. *Self-selection, rather than staff-selection, of activities* and experiences is used in developmentally-appropriate school-age programs. Schedules allow great flexibility for children and youth. Required participation in activities and experiences is limited.

5. Developmentally-appropriate school-age programs use *positive guidance and discipline techniques* to help children and youth achieve self-control and develop their consciences.

6. Environments in developmentally-appropriate school-age programs are *arranged to accommodate children and youth individually, in small groups, and in large groups,* and to facilitate a wide variety of activities and experiences.

7. Activities and experiences offered in developmentally-appropriate school-age programs *contribute to all aspects of a youths' development.*

    a. Activities and experiences foster positive self-concept and a sense of independence.

    b. Activities and experiences encourage children and youth to think, reason, question and experiment.

    c. Activities and experiences enhance physical development and cooperation and promote a healthy view of competition.

    d. Activities and experiences encourage sound health, safety and nutritional practices and the wise use of leisure time.

    e. Activities and experiences encourage awareness of and involvement in the community at large (Albrecht and Plantz, 1991).

This list of guidelines for developmentally-appropriate programming is not exclusive, but it offers a basis for considering this area in the creation of programs.

Two Types of Developmental Appropriateness

It is important that the youth leader consider not only the age appropriateness of activities, but also the individual-appropriateness. Bredekamp (1987) has discussed these two dimensions of developmental appropriateness, as adapted below.

■ **Age Appropriateness.** The term age appropriateness means that programs and activities correspond to the reliable processes and stages of growth and change that occur in youth. For example, the youth leader would not offer activities that require young children to master fine-motor tasks. Age-appropriateness also has been referred to as "stage" appropriateness.

■ **Individual Appropriateness.** Individual appropriateness refers to fact that it is important for the youth leader to be sensitive and responsive to the pattern of growth of each individual youth. Individual appropriateness is an important consideration, since youth can be the same age, yet be at different levels developmentally in terms of mastery of skills.

Planning Age-Appropriate Activities

Both psychologists and sociologists have referred to life stages as a method for grouping people by age and level of development. Youth of elementary school age are often grouped into developmental stages such as six through seven, eight through ten and so on. While it would be incorrect to assume that all youth of a given age have the same developmental characteristics, there is little doubt that as youth pass through developmental stages, they share many of the same characteristics.

Why is it important that activities be age-appropriate? Why should age or developmental level be a factor in determining program activities? As the youth leader plans programs and selects activities, it is important to consider the developmental life stages of youth for the following reasons:

❑   Youth are more likely to *want to participate* in age appropriate activities.

❑   Youth are more likely to *enjoy* those activities.

❑   Youth are more likely to feel a *sense of accomplishment and self-esteem* if activities are related to their developmental stage.

❑   If developmentally-keyed activities are not offered within leisure service programs, *youth may not have an opportunity to engage in them.*

The term "developmentally-appropriate" programming refers to a method for selecting programs and activities that are geared to the developmental characteristics and needs of the youth being served. Since children and youth change dramatically as they mature, activities and programs also need to change and correspond to the needs of each stage of development.

Understanding the characteristics which influence the developmental growth of youth can be used as a basis for determining the most appropriate types of activities to provide.

Ages/Stages of Development

The developmental stages of youth are referred to by various terms. However, in this book, the stages of youth development are referred to as . . .

Early Childhood:	Youth 6-7
Middle Childhood:	Youth 8-10
Early Adolescence:	Youth 11-13
Middle Adolescence:	Youth 14-15
Late Adolescence:	Youth 16-18

Young people develop over time in a fairly predictable way. At certain ages or stages of development, the way in which they perceive themselves, their self-concept and self-images are formed. There are a number of people who have studied youth development and who have ideas about how this development takes place as well as the types of experiences youth should have at each age of their lives for them to develop into strong, healthy, positive, productive and caring adults.

On the following pages are charts that depict developmental characteristics for each of the above age groupings in terms of youths' physical development and health, intellectual development, and social and emotional development as adapted from DeGraaf and DeGraaf, 1994.

DEVELOPMENTAL CHARACTERISTICS OF YOUTH (AGES 6-7)

✓ Age Group Characteristics:

- ❑ Competence in motor skills is increasing
- ❑ Short attention span, deals with here and now
- ❑ Easily frustrated, bored
- ❑ Highly influenced by role models
- ❑ Social rules are important
- ❑ Desire to impress leaders
- ❑ Moves toward peer relationships
- ❑ Moves toward independence
- ❑ An interest in how things are made and work
- ❑ Creativity in art is enjoyed
- ❑ Sensitive to criticism, doesn't accept failure well
- ❑ Easily motivated, eager to try new things
- ❑ Strong desire for affection attention of adults

✓ Implications for Leaders:

- ❑ Instruction in fundamental motor skills is needed
- ❑ Provide early encouragement of health/ fitness
- ❑ Activities should be brief, instructions simple, wide variety
- ❑ Promote positive competition and/or cooperation
- ❑ Be supportive of individual/group successes
- ❑ Function as a good role model
- ❑ Activities should be repeated
- ❑ Activities that promote early academic skill development
- ❑ Activities that promote family relationships

DEVELOPMENTAL CHARACTERISTICS OF YOUTH
(AGES 8-10)

✓ **Age Group Characteristics:**

- ❑ Lengthened Attention Span
- ❑ Spontaneous Emotions
- ❑ Values beginning to emerge
- ❑ Independence from leaders begins
- ❑ Realization of individual limits
- ❑ Starting to get interested in competitive games
- ❑ Impressionable
- ❑ Need for skill development
- ❑ Begins to accept personal responsibility
- ❑ Moves toward group of friends
- ❑ Idolization of significant others (leaders)
- ❑ Eagerness to learn and understand
- ❑ Higher physical stamina
- ❑ Achievement is becoming more important, need praise
- ❑ Like group activity, like to be with same sex members
- ❑ Have rapidly changing interests
- ❑ Easily motivated to try something new

✓ **Implications for Leaders:**

- ❑ Introduce more competitive and cooperative activities
- ❑ Offer higher stamina physical skill activities
- ❑ Provide easy, competitive games
- ❑ Reward or recognize individual/group achievement
- ❑ Occasionally function as a detached leader
- ❑ Emphasis on "hands on" learning, group learning
- ❑ Encourage group members to find answers to questions

DEVELOPMENTAL CHARACTERISTICS OF YOUTH
(AGES 11-13)

✓ **Age Group Characteristics:**

- ❑ Less impulsive
- ❑ High sense of new interests, like clubs
- ❑ Seeking self-identity, may be self-conscious
- ❑ Easily influenced by role models and media
- ❑ Sex identification (boy — girl)
- ❑ Focused on individual relationships and peer approval
- ❑ Emotional feelings can be hidden
- ❑ Higher personal responsibility
- ❑ Interest in group affiliation
- ❑ Further development of independence
- ❑ Ability to develop stable relationships
- ❑ Girls are one year more mature than boys
- ❑ Concerned about physical development, being liked

✓ **Implications for Leaders:**

- ❑ Introduce self-directed activities
- ❑ Cooperative group activities, opportunities for leadership
- ❑ Help youth build social skills, understanding others
- ❑ Provide organized sports
- ❑ Know that girls/boys have different goals/ group affiliations
- ❑ Stress personal responsibility for individual actions
- ❑ Plan and implement activities, then relinquish complete leadership to youth
- ❑ Provide opportunities for planning/decision making
- ❑ Help youth value diversity, take pride in their background

DEVELOPMENTAL CHARACTERISTICS OF YOUTH (AGES 14-15)

✓ **Age Group Characteristics:**

- ❑ Youth are sensitive about development differences
- ❑ Abstract thought regarding events not personally experienced
- ❑ Not yet mature in problem-solving, analytical writing
- ❑ May feel that they are invulnerable
- ❑ May engage in risk-taking behavior
- ❑ Male low-income youth have high drop-out rate
- ❑ Increasing need to make their own decisions
- ❑ Seek out adult role models
- ❑ May become sexually active
- ❑ Struggle between dependence/independence
- ❑ High level of peer pressure/conformity
- ❑ Self-interested

✓ **Implications for Leaders:**

- ❑ Respond to development differences with variety of activities
- ❑ Strategies to encourage kids to stay in school
- ❑ Opportunities to help others/develop feelings of self-worth
- ❑ Have youth help make and enforce rules
- ❑ Exercise, fitness activities promote health, reduce stress
- ❑ Fund-raising activities encourage problem solving, esteem
- ❑ Structure programs/activities to give a sense of risk within structure, e.g. adventure challenge

DEVELOPMENTAL CHARACTERISTICS OF YOUTH (AGES 16-18)

✓ **Age Group Characteristics:**

- ❏ Feeling of invulnerability
- ❏ Need to gain status and power among peers
- ❏ Increased consumption of alcohol
- ❏ Increased capacity for abstract thought, reason, logic
- ❏ Looking for purpose/meaning in life
- ❏ May have after-school jobs
- ❏ Lessened conflict with parents, as independence increases
- ❏ Strong sexual feelings
- ❏ Developing beliefs, values, self-concept

✓ **Implications for Leaders:**

- ❏ Offer opportunities for meaningful interaction/bonding.
- ❏ Offer opportunities for contributing/helping others.
- ❏ Demonstrate leader — participant trust.
- ❏ Be aware that youth have interest in both same-sex friendships, as well as opposite-sex friendships.
- ❏ Offer opportunities for exploring career options, values, beliefs, issues.
- ❏ Encourage decision-making, leadership, problem-solving. Offer structured risk-taking activities.
- ❏ Structure programs/activities to give a sense of freedom, influence and autonomy.
- ❏ Offer opportunities for physical activity.
- ❏ Offer opportunities for meaningful creative expression.

A Final Note

There are opportunities at each life age/stage of development for youth to grow and develop. Often, these opportunities for growth, if not achieved, may not again be available. It is important that the leader be aware of the opportunities for development that occur throughout the lives of youth, in order to be able to respond effectively.

Personal Notes:
Life Ages/Stages of Youth

What are some of techniques you should use in planning programs and activities that are developmentally-appropriate and individual-appropriate?

1.   Group children together in same-age groups or in mixed-age groups?

Both types of groupings should be used to develop peer relations and social skills, keeping in mind safety factors and that youth should feel a sense of competence.

2.   Select activities based on your expertise or allow children to select activities?

It is important to allow youth to have influence in selecting programs and activities.

3.   Structure activities so that they are conducted individually? In small groups? In large groups?

All three. Also offer a wide variety of activities and programs.

4.   Plan activities that are age-appropriate? Individual-appropriate?

It is important that activities be individual-appropriate; children may be the same age, but be at different developmental stages.

References

Albrecht, K.M. and M.C. Plantz (1991). *Developmentally- Appropriate Practice in School-Age Child Care Programs.* Alexandria, VA: American Home Economics Association.

Bredekamp, S. (Ed.) (1987). *Developmentally-Appropriate Practice in Early Childhood Programs Serving Children from Birth to Age 8.* Washington, D.C.: National Association for the Education of Young Children.

DeGraaf, D.G. and K.H. DeGraaf. (1994). *U.S. Army Youth Services Training Guide: Planning and Supervising Camp Programs.* Cedar Falls, IA: University of Northern Iowa.

Erikson, E. H. (1963). *Childhood and Society.* New York: Norton.

CHAPTER 7

YOUTH DEVELOPMENT COMPETENCIES/NEEDS

What are the developmental needs of youth? What competencies should youth master in order to become healthy, positive adults? These are complex questions that may challenge the youth leader. It is important for the youth leader to have an understanding of what the overarching goals are for youth, in order to plan effectively and place programs and services into proper context.

In this chapter, information will be presented for youth leaders regarding the developmental competencies that youth must acquire in order to become healthy, positive adults. Youth must gain certain experiences in order to develop appropriately. In addition, youth have needs that must be met for them to achieve a sense of self-esteem, belonging, well-being and achievement. Leaders working with youth have traditionally contributed to their development; however, this has often been done without definitive statements or direction concerning outcomes. This portion of the book will provide a focus for the work of the youth leader tied to a concrete foundation of development.

As a result of reviewing this chapter you will be able to:

▶ Gain an understanding of the five youth development competencies that youth must acquire to become healthy, positive adults.

▶ Develop an understanding of the ten (10) basic needs of youth that are fundamental to survival and healthy development.

▶ Increase the impact of programming by incorporating youth development competencies and basic youth needs.

YOUTH DEVELOPMENT COMPETENCIES/NEEDS

As youth grow and develop through childhood and adolescence, there are certain skills that they must acquire in order to develop positively and to become healthy adults. Many of these experiences and skills can be found within recreation programs and activities.

The Role of the Leader in Youth Development

Youth development is, in large part, in the hands of youths themselves. The youth leader can't get inside of young people and motivate them. It is like the story of the oak tree and the acorn. We can't get inside of an acorn and make it grow. But we can make sure that it has enough sunlight, water and good soil and then hope that it grows and develops into a strong and healthy tree.

In the same way, the youth leader can create an environment and climate that encourages youth development by providing personal support, opportunity for involvement and learning, well-planned programs, materials and equipment with which youth development can take place. Youth development is an ongoing process to which youth themselves must be committed and involved.

Helping You Choose Youth Development Objectives

What are the youth development objectives that you will promote as a youth leader? There are many organizations that serve youth and that foster youth development, called *youth-serving agencies*. Each of these youth-serving agencies has purposes and objectives for the work they do. For example, the objectives of *Camp Fire Boys and Girls* programs are to promote individual accomplishment, creativity, cultural and environmental appreciation, citizenship, service and self-reliance.

By looking at the goals and objectives of other organizations, you will get an idea of the types of youth development objectives that can be promoted. Youth-serving organizations that are committed to youth development all have youth development objectives, toward which they focus their efforts.

Following is an adapted list of youth development objectives identified by nine youth-serving agencies from a report by the Center for Youth Development and Policy Research (Pittman and Write, 1991), to which *Camp Adventure*™ Youth Services program objectives have been added.

- The programs of the *American Red Cross* are designed to contribute to the development of 1) health promotion, 2) leadership, 3) community service, and 4) international understanding.

- The *Boy Scouts'* activities are designed to 1) build character, 2) foster citizenship, 3) developmental, moral and physical fitness.

- The *Boys and Girls Clubs'* activities promote health, social, educational, vocational and character development.

- *Camp Fire Boys and Girls* programs promote individual accomplishment, creativity, cultural and environmental appreciation, citizenship, service and self-reliance.

- *Girl Scouts'* programs have four goals: 1) to develop self-potential, 2) relating to others, 3) developing values, 4) contributing to society.

- *Girls Inc.* has defined six core content areas for its programs that address 1) careers and life planning, 2) health and sexuality, 3) leadership and community action, 4) sports and adventure, 5) self-reliance and life skills, 6) culture and heritage.

- The *National 4-H Clubs'* programs are designed to foster competency, partnerships, coping skills and contributory skills.

- The *YMCA's* youth development concept incorporates five key components: 1) self-esteem, 2) personal health, 3) employment skills and career goals, 4) education and training, 5) leadership and service.

- The *YWCA* core program emphasizes five (5) major themes: 1) empowerment, 2) health promotion, 3) youth development, 4) family life, 5) community leadership.

- The *Camp Adventure*™ Youth Services program is designed to create "magic moments for children that last a lifetime" by developing, *with* youth, activities that promote social bonding, health and fitness, youth leadership, independence and life skills.

FIVE DEVELOPMENTAL OBJECTIVES/ COMPETENCIES THAT YOUTH MUST ACQUIRE

Now that you have had a chance to look at what *other* organizations do in terms of selecting and promoting specific youth development objectives, what types of objectives will *you* promote? Why?

Five basic areas of youth development objectives or *competencies* have been developed based on a review of the youth development areas that are seen as being important by youth-serving organizations. *Five competencies that youth should acquire in order to be successful as adults,* as adapted from Pittman (1991), include. . .

❑   **Health/physical competence.** Youth need to have *good current health status* and appropriate knowledge, attitudes and *behaviors to ensure future health* (exercise, good diet, nutrition).

❑   **Personal/social competence.** It is important that youth gain: *intrapersonal skills* (ability to understand personal emotions, have self-discipline); *interpersonal skills* (ability to work with others, develop friendships and relationships through communication, cooperation, empathizing, negotiating); *coping/system skills* (ability to adapt, assume responsibility); and *judgment skills* (plan, make decisions, solve problems).

❑   **Cognitive/creative competence.** Youth need to develop a broad base of *knowledge,* ability to appreciate/participate in areas of *creative expression,* good oral, written *language skills, problem-solving and analytical skills,* ability to learn/*interest in learning and achieving.*

❑   **Vocational competence.** It is important for youth to develop a broad understanding/*awareness of vocational (and avocational) options* and of steps to act on choices; adequate preparation for career, understanding of value and function of work/ leisure.

❑   **Citizenship competencies (ethics and preparation).** Youth need to understand their *nation's and community's history and values,* and *desire to contribute* to nation and community.

As youth move toward mastering these areas, they also progress in their feelings of achievement and self esteem. Youth need to be good at something in order to feel good about themselves.

Five Competencies that Youth Should Master to Become Successful Adults

CITIZENSHIP COMPETENCE

• Understand Nation/Community History/Values

PERSONAL/SOCIAL COMPETENCE

• Understand Personal Emotions
• Develop Friendships
• Self-Discipline
• Coping/System Skills
• Judgement Skills

COGNITIVE CREATIVE COMPETENCE

• Broad Base of Knowledge
• Creative Expression
• Language Skills
• Interest in Learning

HEALTH/PHYSICAL COMPETENCE

• Food/Current Health Knowledge/Skills to Ensure Future Health

VOCATIONAL COMPETENCE

• Awareness of Vocational/Career Options
• Understand Value of Work/Leisure

A 1989 Carnegie Report also reports on youth development competencies, using a different, but similar model. This report cites the five goals of healthy adolescent development as cognitive, social, physical, emotional, and moral development as outlined below.

Cognitive Development
- Expand knowledge;
- Develop critical thinking and reasoning skills; and
- Experience competence through academic achievement.

Social Development
- Increase communication and negotiation skills;
- Increase capacity for meaningful relationships with peers and adults; and
- Explore adult rights and responsibilities.

Physical Development
- Begin to mature physically and to understand changes that come with puberty;
- Increase movement skills through physical activity;
- Develop habits that promote lifelong physical fitness; and
- Learn to take and manage appropriate physical risks.

Emotional Development
- Develop a sense of personal identity;
- Develop a sense of personal autonomy and control; and
- Develop coping, decision-making, and stress-management skills.

Moral Development
- Develop personal values;
- Develop a sense of accountability and responsibility in relation to the larger society; and
- Apply values and beliefs in meaningful ways.

This report cites the importance of investment in early childhood and adolescent programs.

WHAT ARE THE BASIC NEEDS OF YOUTH?

Not only is it important for the youth leader to help youth acquire experience and skills related to the developmental competencies, but youth have certain basic needs that also must be met. There are basic needs that youth have that are fundamental for survival and healthy development.

Various organizations, individuals and groups have attempted to identity the basic needs of youth. Following are ten (10) basic human needs of youth as adapted from Pittman (1991) and Scales (1991). Youth programs and services help meet these developmental needs:

❑   **A Need for Positive Social Interaction.** Youth want to belong, and need opportunities to form positive social relationships with adults and peers.

❑   **A Need for Safety, Structure and Clear Limits.** Expectations, structure and boundaries are important for youth, so that they feel secure and also have a clear picture of the areas that they can/cannot explore.

❑   **A Need for Belonging and Meaningful Involvement in Family, School, Community.** Youth have a desire to be a part of and to participate in activities related to their families, their schools and their communities.

❑   **A Need for Creative Expression.** Youth need opportunities to express to others who they are and how they feel. Music, writing, sports, cooking or other activities help to achieve this goal.

❑   **A Need for Feeling Self-Worth/Giving to Others.** Involvement in meaningful and worthwhile effort related to larger goals is extremely important to youth.

❑   **A Need for Physical Activity.** Youth have tremendous energy and require a great deal of physical activity and time for fun.

❑   **A Need to Feel a Sense of Independence, Autonomy and Control.** Youth have a desire to mature, become more independent and to exert some control and influence over their lives.

❑   **A Need for Closeness in Relationships.** Youth need opportunities to form close relationships with peers and adults. They also have a need for relationships with caring adult role models.

❑   **A Need for Feeling a Sense of Competence and Achievement.** It is important for youth to have opportunities to achieve success and to receive recognition.

❑   **A Need for a Sense of Individualism, Identity, and Self-Definition.** Youth need to have opportunities to become individuals and to define their sense of identity and self-concept, based on positive input from others.

This list of developmental needs of youth gives the youth leader guidelines for the types of interaction, activities and programs that youth need, and the ways that programs and services should be guided.

Youth leaders who organize programs and services in a manner that allow youth to have input, involvement and ownership, to have a sense of achievement and recognition, to have opportunities for creative expression and physical activity and to have opportunities for social interaction, will find that youth not only will be likely to participate, but that they will show evidence of benefit from their participation.

Ten Basic Needs of Youth

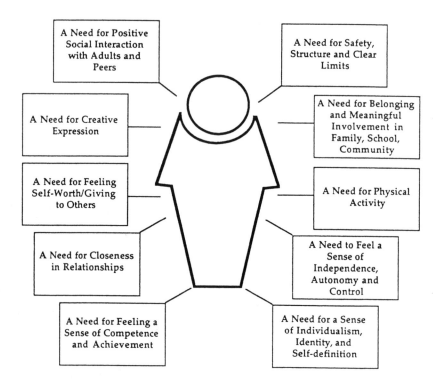

A Need for Positive Social Interaction with Adults and Peers

A Need for Safety, Structure and Clear Limits

A Need for Creative Expression

A Need for Belonging and Meaningful Involvement in Family, School, Community

A Need for Feeling Self-Worth/Giving to Others

A Need for Physical Activity

A Need for Closeness in Relationships

A Need to Feel a Sense of Independence, Autonomy and Control

A Need for Feeling a Sense of Competence and Achievement

A Need for a Sense of Individualism, Identity, and Self-definition

A Final Note

Principles of youth development offer a foundation upon which the work of a youth services organization can be predicated. We can think of youth development as an integrating concept for the work of youth services organizations, as well as other organizations that serve youth. Youth development is a construct that reflects the needs of youth, while at the same time providing direction for youth as they strive to gain the competencies necessary to become healthy, positive, productive adults.

Personal Notes:
Ages/Stages of Development

Using the list of age group characteristics below, determine what programs and activities you can offer for this age group, that will respond to their needs.

✓ Age Group Characteristics (Youth 11-13)

- ❑ Less impulsive
- ❑ High sense of new interests, like fan (or other) clubs
- ❑ Seeking self-identity, may be self-conscious
- ❑ Easily influenced by role models and media
- ❑ Sex identification (boy — girl)
- ❑ Focused on individual relationships and peer approval
- ❑ Emotional feelings can be hidden
- ❑ Higher personal responsibility
- ❑ Interest in group affiliation
- ❑ Further development of independence
- ❑ Ability to develop stable relationships
- ❑ Girls are one year more mature than boys
- ❑ Concerned about physical development, being liked

✓ Implications for Leaders:

- ❑ Introduce self-directed activities
- ❑ Cooperative group activities, opportunities for leadership
- ❑ Help youth build social skills, understanding others
- ❑ Provide organized sports
- ❑ Know that girls/boys have different goals/ group affiliations
- ❑ Stress personal responsibility for individual actions.

□   Plan and implement activities — then
relinquish complete activity control and
creativity to youth
□   Provide opportunities for planning/decision
making
□   Helping youth value diversity, take pride in
their background

Program/Activity Ideas:

_____

_____

_____

_____

References

Carnegie Council on Adolescent Development. (1992). *A Matter of Time: Risk and Opportunity in the Non-School Hours.* New York: Carnegie Corporation.

Pittman, K.J. and M. Wright (1991). *A Rationale for Enhancing the Role of the Non-School Voluntary Sector in Youth Development.* New York: Center for Youth Development and Policy Research.

Pittman, K.J. (1991). *Promoting Youth Development: Strengthening the Role of Youth Serving and Community Organizations.* New York: Center for Youth Development and Policy Research.

Scales, P. (1991). *A Portrait of Youth Adolescents in the 1990s.* Carborro, N C : Center for Early Adolescence.

CHAPTER 8

VALUES DEVELOPMENT

Youth leaders do not work in a value-free environment. In fact, youth services organizations are deliberately designed with the intention of promoting a specific set of values, beliefs and ideas. Common values often promoted by youth serving organizations include citizenship, health and fitness, concern for the environment, fair play, contribution to others, self-awareness and development, as well as other values. Youth leaders transmit values that reflect the goals of their organization and, as such, are in the "business" of values development. Values development involves not only transmitting specific values to youth, but also helping youth to reflect upon and sort out their beliefs and values related to life events and experiences.

In this chapter, information is offered to help the youth leader assist youth to consider their values. The leader promotes certain values through his/her interactions, and is in a position to help youth think about and clarify their values. It has often been said that we have a crisis of values among youth in American society. Youth leaders play a prominent role in helping youth today consider how they are living their lives, what is important to them, and what types of values they see as being important to their future endeavors.

As a result of reading this chapter you will be able to:

▶ Gain an understanding of the role of the leader in transmitting values to youth.

▶ Develop knowledge of some of the basic or core values that may be encouraged by the youth leader.

▶ Gain information regarding strategies that you can use to help youth clarify their values.

VALUES DEVELOPMENT

Youth leaders, both intentionally or unintentionally, transmit values to youth and others of the public with whom they interact (Edginton & Edginton, 1992). There is no such thing as a value-free program, activity or event. It is important for youth leaders to be aware of the way in which they impact upon the values of youth. The leader's language, dress, attitudes, ideas and behavior toward others, as well as other factors, impact upon the youth they serve.

The leader not only promotes certain values through his/ her interactions, but also is in a position to help youth think about and clarify their values. In every program, activity or event, leaders who are aware of the tools that can be used can help youth clarify their values in a positive and constructive manner. Following are topics discussed in this chapter.

The Role of the Leader in Values Development
- ❏   What are Values?
- ❏   What is Values Development?
- ❏   The Role of the Leader

Promoting Basic Values
- ❏   Youth Development
- ❏   Independence and Responsibility
- ❏   Leadership
- ❏   Citizenship/Country
- ❏   Respect for Others
- ❏   Peer Pressure/Individuality
- ❏   Positive Enjoyment of Life
- ❏   Trust/Communication
- ❏   Commitment/Industriousness
- ❏   Teamwork/Competitiveness

Helping Youth Consider Their Values
- ❏   Value Clarifying Statements
- ❏   Value Clarification Strategies

THE ROLE OF THE LEADER IN
VALUES DEVELOPMENT

What are values? Should the youth leader help youth think about and consider their values? If so, how would the leader do this? These are some of the questions that the leader will need to consider in relation to the issue of values.

What Are Values?

Values are *principles or guidelines that individuals believe to be important in life.* Values are freely chosen after some consideration and, once developed, are acted upon. Very often, values determine the course of action that an individual will take, and will influence the way in which they direct their energy and resources.

What is Values Development?

Values development is *based on the idea that the leader can help youth develop and define their values through use of selected methods.* No organization or leader is without strong values. Therefore, the leader and his or her organization *will* impact upon the formulation of values by youth in some manner.

With this in mind, it is important for the organization and the leader to consider the issue of values, and to ensure that the impact upon the values of youth occurs in a knowledgeable, beneficial and organized way.

The Role of the Leader

Should the leader promote certain values? Or, are values such an individual matter that the leader should attempt to be "value free" as much as possible? *There is no such thing as a value-free environment, youth leaders always impart values.* Therefore, the leader should carefully review and consider the types of values he or she will promote within the program setting.

In addition, the leader should determine the organization's values. Often they are contained in a vision statement. It is important that the leader support the values of the organization. The leader should have an intentional, informed role in regard to values development, rather than an unintentional, hit or miss approach.

PROMOTING BASIC, "CORE" VALUES

Following are a number of "core" values that the leader may want to promote within programs, activities and events. This list is by no means complete or exclusive. These values are intended to represent basic actions of consideration, development and integrity.

As youth develop these types of values, they will become more independently functioning, independently thinking individuals.

Independence/Responsibility

The leader can greatly influence the values of youth in terms of becoming more independent. There are numerous *opportunities within leisure programs, activities and events to allow youth to act independently and responsibly,* and to assume responsibility in greater proportion over a period of time.

Does the leader allow youth an opportunity to make mistakes and learn from mistakes? Does the leader allow them to become involved in the planning and execution of programs, activities and events in a manner that promotes independence and responsibility? Or, does the leader "do everything" for youth, and place them in a dependent role? Are youth made aware of their responsibility as people to one another, to the leader, to their parents?

Peer Pressure/Individuality

The leader may have an opportunity to help youth shape values related to the issue of conformity versus individuality. All youth are confronted with issues and situations in which they must make decisions about *whether to conform to group pressure or peer pressure, or whether to act as an individual* and be true to personal values.

The leader, including leaders working with teens, may have an opportunity to help youth clarify their values in this regard. The leader can use such phrases as "How do you feel when you go along with the group against your best judgment?" "Do you think it is important to be true to yourself and to trust your own judgment?"

Leadership

Closely tied to independence and responsibility are values associated with leadership. Leaders can be "made." That is, leadership qualities will emerge if the youth leader promotes values related to leadership as being positive and fun, encourages mutual support and structures opportunities for leadership. As youth are given *opportunities for leadership and responsibility*, the leader can also reinforce the idea that leaders have a responsibility to model positive, constructive values.

Citizenship/Country

It is important for the leader to consider values related to citizenship and country. Leaders must take seriously their responsibility in this area, recognizing that their opinions, ideas and values may strongly shape the perceptions of youth.

The leader has a responsibility to maintain a level of *respect and positiveness in discussions that occur about the value of the democratic process and the role and responsibility of citizens in a democracy.*

Respect for Others

An important value that the leader can help youth develop is a sense of respect and consideration for others. Respect is closely tied to responsibility — the idea that *we have responsibilities to one another, to the group, to the leader, to our parents and others,* to consider their needs as well as our own.

The individual has a responsibility to recognize that his or her behavior has consequences and will impact upon others either positively or negatively, and to think about the choice that he/she makes in this regard.

Youth Development

Most youth leaders promote values related to youth development. Youth should be encouraged *to develop themselves physically, socially, emotionally and cognitively.* Values related to physical fitness, healthy lifestyle, learning, creativity, exploration should be encouraged by the youth leader.

The leader can ask youth clarifying questions related to youth development that help youth shape their values. For example, "How does it make you feel when you exercise?" "Do you like to be creative?" "What is your favorite type of sport?" "Is there something special that you like to learn about?" "How can you find out more information about that subject?"

Positive Enjoyment of Life

Life is great! Life has adventures, surprises and fun! The leader has a choice of whether to help youth formulate *values regarding the positiveness of life,* or whether to pass along values that speak of life as problem oriented, negative, and depressing.

All leaders will have problems related to programming, behavior problems, and personal problems. However, the way the leader interacts with youth in terms of solving problems will communicate to youth either a positive orientation that problems are challenges to be overcome and learned from, or a negative orientation that problems are insurmountable, never-ending obstacles. Do you have a positive outlook on life?

Trust/Communication

The perceptions and values of youth about other people, and their trust in other people, is influenced by the way that they are treated by "relevant others;" that is, people who are meaningful to them in their lives. Youth leaders with whom they come in contact are often in this category.

If the leader is an individual that communicates *values related to trust, open communication and unconditional concern and respect,* then youth will use this information to help them formulate their impressions about the world. Do you transmit values that indicate that you can be trusted to "be there" for your youth, or do you withdraw support and care depending on the situation, your mood and their behavior?

Teamwork/Competitiveness

Within youth programs, there is an opportunity for the youth leader to promote values related to teamwork and competitiveness. *Healthy competition, based upon support of one another and teamwork* are values that the leader can support.

Fair play and teamwork are issues that come up frequently within youth activities. Often there are values promoted that suggest "Win at any cost," rather than, "Play fair play hard, nobody loses."

The youth leader *will* transmit values to youth, so it is important the leader give some thought to the types of values he/she wants to impart to youth. Following are some additional values that the leader may want to incorporate formally or informally into programs.

Caring	Equality	Peace	Compassion
Courtesy	Critical Inquiry	Freedom	Integrity
Knowledge	Loyalty	Objectivity	Order
Tolerance	Truth	Justice	Human Dignity

PROMOTING VALUES
WITHIN PROGRAM THEMES

It is possible and desirable to promote values that relate to themed activities, theme weeks or theme months. Values that are coordinated with program themes may be meaningful to youth since discussion of them occurs in context; that is, the values relate to the theme. This portion of the program guide contains recommendations of values that can be tied to various themes.

Six theme weeks used within the *Camp Adventure*™ youth services program are presented in this portion of the program guide, with potential value areas that relate to the different themes. This list is not complete, there are other values that could relate to these areas. In addition, values can be a part of youth programs that do not have a theme. The six theme weeks presented here are:

- ❑   Jammin Through the Jungle

- ❑   Fourth of July Spirit

- ❑   Grandslam Sports Spectacular

- ❑   Ramblin' Around the World

- ❑   Space Raiders and Cosmic Invaders

- ❑   Super Sleuths and Spies Like Us

In using theme weeks as a vehicle to promote certain basic or core values, it is important the youth leader set the stage for youth to consider values, but allow them to form their own conclusions regarding values. In other words, the youth leader should allow youth to consider values, analyze and evaluate them, and then adopt them or not as their choice.

Values: "Jammin' Through the Jungle" Theme Week:

- ❑   Preserving the environment

- ❑   Saving the rainforest

- ❑   Recycling

- ❑   Preserving endangered species

- ❑   Global warming

Values: "Fourth of July Spirit" Theme Week:

❏   Importance of being free/independent.

❏   The need to do what youth know is right even if others don't agree.

❏   Importance of loyalty to country.

❏   Importance of responsibility as citizens.

❏   Opportunity to learn other values tied to our nation's history and development.

Values: "Grandslam Sports Spectacular" Theme Week:

❏   Importance of being physically fit, having a healthy body and eating properly for energy and stamina.

❏   The importance of developing lifelong leisure skills.

❏   Chance to develop interpersonal/teamwork skills.

❏   A focus on personal best, as opposed to outside standards.

❏   Understanding the difference between healthy, fun competition and "win at all costs."

Values: "Ramblin' Around the World" Theme Week:

❏   Emphasizing the need for peace and harmony within the world.

❐   Understanding that people are different, but also the same.

❐   Realizing that our world is richer as a result of different types of people.

❐   Becoming motivated to find out more about other people/countries.

❐   Realizing that there are basic values that all people have; the importance of family, caring about others, loyalty to country, honesty, responsibility.

Values: "Space Raiders and Cosmic Invaders" Theme Week:

❐   Understanding the importance of exploring new frontiers.

❐   Gaining an appreciation for values related to learning and   achieving, discovery and science.

❐   Understanding our world in terms of both its scientific and its unknown/spiritual nature.

❐   Gaining an appreciation of the need to protect our planet.

❐   Understanding the importance of finding things that you enjoy to do and then pursuing them.

❐   Considering the future and our place in the continuum of the centuries.

Values: "Super Sleuths and Spies Like Us" Theme Week:

❑   Using problem-solving/analytical skills. The joy of figuring things out.

❑   Learning that in real life it is important not to have secrets, but to be open with people so people can know you and help you.

❑   Learning that it is good to help one another and figure things out as a team.

❑   Experiencing the joy of creative expression, storytelling, creative writing.

Although values can be incorporated into themed weeks, themed events, as well as non-themed activities, it is important that education occur with a small "e." It is important for the youth leader to understand the potential for and impact upon youth development; however, the leader's goal should always be fun, enjoyment, excitement and exceeding expectations.

Every *organization* has values to which it subscribes and which it promotes. For example most leisure service organizations promote programs that are positive, wholesome, constructive, and developmentally-sound.

With the assistance of the leader, youth can consider and develop values that they will subscribe to throughout their lives. In addition, they can be helped to think critically about their ideas, prior to accepting values as their own. They may also sort out which of their values is more important to them.

HELPING YOUTH CONSIDER THEIR VALUES

The leader not only can choose to support certain basic values, he or she can also *help youth review, evaluate and consider their values.* There are certain prescribed statements that can be used by the leader to help youth think about their ideas, feelings and values related to them.

For example, a leader might ask a youth who has expressed an idea questions such as "How do you know that is right?" "Is that important to you?" "Have you felt that way for very long?" The leader is able to provoke thought in this way. Following are several ideas that can be used by the leader to help youth think about and clarify their values.

Value Clarifying

There are a number of statements that can be used by the leader to help youth think about and clarify their values. *These statements can be used to talk to youth in a brief, thought- provoking manner* so that they begin to focus more clearly on who they are, what they believe in and what they want to do.

Following is a sample of several conversations that might occur between the leader and youth using value clarifying statements.

Leader:	Amy, you say you enjoy arts and crafts?
Amy:	Yes, I like it a lot.
Leader:	What are some of the things you like most about arts and crafts?
Leader:	John, you say you like space and rockets?
John:	I think they are a lot of fun.
Leader:	What do you think you can do to find out more about them?
Heather:	I love to play soccer.
Leader:	Oh, do you play soccer a lot?
Heather:	Yes, I play on a team.
Leader:	Is soccer important to you?

You will notice that these conversations are brief and may not result in a conclusive comment. However, they have the effect of generating thought and interest. Youth are encouraged to consider their statements in a thoughtful way.

Value Clarifying Statements

The leader can *use value clarifying statements to help youth consider and act upon their values.* Following is a list of value clarifying statements as adapted by Purpel and Ryan (1976) that can be used by the leader.

- Is this something you prize?
- Are you glad about that?
- How did you feel when that happened?
- Did you consider any alternatives?
- Have you felt this way for a long time?
- Was that something you yourself selected or chose?
- Did you do anything about that idea?
- Can you give me some examples of that idea?
- Would you really do that, or are you just talking?
- Have you thought much about that idea?
- What other possibilities are there?
- Is that very important to you?
- Would you like to tell others about your idea?
- How do you know it is right?

As you can see, there are a number of questions that the leader can ask that will provoke thought among youth. Youth often hear or see a person who transmits a certain value and they accept it without question or consideration.

These types of statements encourage youths to question and evaluate their ideas and values, rather than accepting them point blank.

Value Clarifying Guidelines

Guidelines for Using Statements. As the leader uses these types of clarifying statements, he or she should keep in mind the following guidelines as adapted from Purpel and Ryan (1976).

- The leader should not moralize, give values or evaluate the youth's response.

- The responsibility is on the youth to examine his/her values.
- The youth *may not* choose to examine his/her values.
- The points are short, they are not intended to be long discussions.
- The statements should relate to each individual
- The leader uses these periodically, not all the time.
- There are no "right" answers.
- The statements should be used creatively.

Value Clarifying Strategies

In addition, to value clarifying statements, there are *value clarifying strategies that the leader can use to encourage youth to think about and consider their values.* For example, youth can be asked to draw a "coat of arms" and include things that are important to them on the diagram.

There are a number of value clarifying strategies that can be used by the leader working with youth. These strategies represent more direct action on the part of the leader, as opposed to the informal value clarification that often occurs within the leisure setting.

A Final Note

Youth are exposed to a variety of values in our society today. Youth leaders may work with youth to help them review, evaluate, and clarify their personal values. Individuals who develop clear values, chosen freely, have a firm basis for future action; they know what they value, what is important to them, what they believe in, and where they are headed. Most youth service organizations have at their core a set of values in which they believe and that they want to transmit to youth. As such, youth leaders serve a vital function in the values development of youth.

The Role of the Leader in Values Development

A Personal Coat of Arms

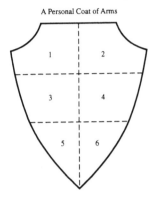

Each participant is asked to draw a shield shape in preparation for making a personal coat of arms. The leader could explain the historical significance of shields and coats of arms, but the purpose of this strategy is to help participants learn the importance of publicly affirming what we believe.

The coat of arms shield is divided into six sections (see figure). The leader makes it clear that words are to be used only in the sixth block. All the others are to contain pictures. He or she stresses that it is not an art lesson. Only crude stick figures, and so on, need to be used. Then he or she tells what is to go in each of the six sections.

1. Draw two pictures, one to represent something you are very good at and one to show something you want to be good at.

2. Make a picture to show one of your values from which you would never budge. This is one about which you have extremely strong feelings and that you might never give up.

3. Draw a picture to show a value by which your family lives. Make it one that everyone in your family would probably agree is one of their most important values.

4. In this block imagine that you could achieve anything you wanted and that whatever you tried to do would be a success. What would you strive to do?

5. Use this block to show one of the values you wished all people would believe and certainly one in which you believe very deeply.

6. In the last block, you can use words. Use four words that you would like people to say about you behind your back.

Following the creation of the coats of arms, the leader might want to let participants share them among themselves in small groups.

Source: Adapted from Sidney B. Simon, "Values Clarification vs. Indoctrination." in David Purpel and Kevin Ryan, eds. Moral Education: It Comes with the Territory. Berkeley, CA: McCutchin Publishing Corp.

Personal Notes:
Values Development

Please examine the list of 20 values below, and rank them in order of their importance to you. Enter the value that is most important to you first.

Caring	Equality	Peace
Honesty	Integrity	Communication
Knowledge	Loyalty	Individuality
Truth	Justice	Trust
Leadership	Citizenship	Freedom
Respect for Others	Teamwork	Responsibility
Independence	Contribution to others	

1.	11.
2.	12.
3.	13.
4.	14.
5.	15.
6.	16.
7.	17.
8.	18.
9.	19.
10.	20.

Now that you have examined your own values, how will you assist youth to examine their values? During which programs or activities could you encourage youth to consider the five values that you think are most important? List five program ideas that could help youth consider the five values that you think are most important.

———————————   ———————————

———————————   ———————————

———————————

References

Edginton, C.R. and S. Edginton (1993). The Role of Camp Counselors in Values Development for Youth. *Camping Magazine,65* (4).

Purpel, D. and K. Ryan (1976). *Moral Education: It Comes With the Territory.* Berkeley, CA: McCutcheon Publishing Corporation.

PART III

CREATING & PLANNING YOUTH-CENTERED PROGRAMS

CHAPTER 9

THE YOUTH-CENTERED PLANNING PROCESS

The planning of programs and services for youth is a challenging, yet rewarding, endeavor for the youth leader. Programs and activities are the vehicles through which youth development takes place. They provide opportunities for values to be developed, beliefs to be considered and behaviors to be shaped. The program planning process works best when youth are empowered to participate in the process. A youth-centered program planning process is one that not only involves youth, but has as its core focus the needs of youth.

This chapter of the book offers an overview of a six-step process for planning youth programs. Included in the presentation will be a discussion of ways in which to assess needs, plan program goals and objectives, develop program format and design, and, ultimately, implement and evaluate services. This brief chapter will present an overview of the complete planning process, which will then be described in terms of each of its steps in subsequent chapters.

As a result of review of this chapter you will be able to:

▶ Understand the components of the planning process and how to use them in a manner that meets the needs of youth and offers them opportunities for leadership.

▶ Gain a preliminary overview of the methods that can be used to plan programs, including, assessing the needs of youth during preparation and initial planning, setting program goals and objectives, selecting a program format and program design and managing program flow, program supervision and evaluation.

PLANNING PROCESS OVERVIEW

Why is it important for the youth leader to follow a particular process in terms of planning and carrying out programs? Why can't the leader just "wing it" and decide, on the spot, what activities and programs to provide? What are the advantages to the leader of using a planning process?

Although there is a need for spontaneity in youth programs, flexibility must occur within a carefully structured and planned program in order to provide well-organized, safe, consistent, reliable, age-appropriate and relevant programs. Programs must also be consistent with the goals, rules and policies of the sponsoring organization.

This program planning method places importance on involving youth and considering youths' needs. As a result, it is called the "Youth-Centered" Program Planning Process. Following is a list of the steps of this planning process:

❑ Preparation

❑ Initial Planning

❑ Program Goals and Objectives

❑ Program Design/Program Formats

❑ Program Flow/Supervision

❑ Evaluation

The "Youth-Centered" Program Planning diagram or model has six (6) steps that range from preparation or pre-planning as the first step, to program evaluation as the last step. Following is a brief overview of each of these steps. This will be followed by a detailed discussion of each step.

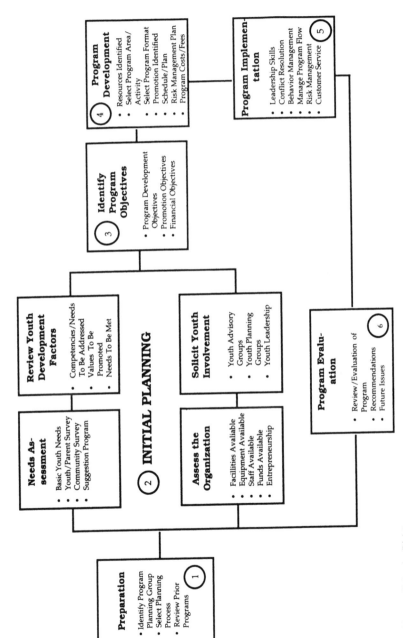

Youth-Centered Program Planning

Preparation

The preparation phase of the planning process involves three activities: 1) deciding who will be in the planning group; 2) deciding what process (what steps) will be used to plan programs; and 3) reviewing helpful information such as manuals, brochures or other information that shows the types of programs that were carried out in the past.

Initial Planning

In the initial planning step of the program planning process, the youth leader focuses on two activities: 1) determining what resources and facilities are available for programs; and 2) attempting to plan to meet the needs of youth by involving youth in planning, assessing the needs of youth, and review of written material in the area of youth development competencies and needs.

Identify Program Objectives

It is important for the youth leader to identify program goals and objectives. What is it that the youth leader hopes to see youth accomplish as a result of participation in programs and activities? Specific behavioral objectives may be written that outline the particular physical behaviors that youth will exhibit as a result of participation.

Program Development

Once the leader has linked the needs of youth with the program's objectives, program development takes place. Within the program development step of the planning process, the youth leader will focus on selecting the program area, specific type of program, program format, facilities, setting, equipment and supplies, staffing, cost, promotion and risk management.

Program Implementation

Connecting with youth to provide meaningful programs is a focus in this step of the process. In addition, managing the flow of the program so that it achieves the desired result and supervising other elements of the program are involved in this step. Finally, promoting youth leadership during the implementation of the program is an important consideration.

Evaluation

This step in the program planning process includes two activities: 1) formative evaluation, which deals with evaluating the program as it is still taking place and making corrections; and 2) summative evaluation, which involves evaluation of the program after it is over and then making recommendations for future programs.

A Final Note

There is no substitute for program planning. Effective planning is the key to success. Planning enables youth leaders to visualize an event and the way in which programs will unfold, as well as the resources to be used. The youth leader will be made more effective and efficient with comprehensive planning.

CHAPTER 10

PREPARATION FOR
PROGRAM PLANNING

As a youth leader, you will be responsible for planning and developing program services. This chapter of the book presents the first step of the program planning process — preparation or pre-planning. The preparation step in program planning is involved with deciding upon your planning group, choosing your planning process and reviewing prior programs and services.

As a result of reading this chapter, you will be able to:

▶ Understand the importance of laying the groundwork for program planning.

▶ Increase the impact of planning by choosing a planning group that is representative of specific planning needs.

▶ Gain an understanding of the basic components that should be included in a planning process.

Following is the *preparation step* as it appears in the program planning diagram:

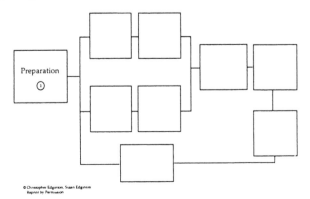

The preparation phase of the planning process is involved with pre-planning. The activities during this part of the planning process are related to set up, including the following:

❑   Deciding who will be in the planning group.

❑   Deciding what process (what steps) will be used to plan programs.

❑   Reviewing information regarding prior programs.

Choosing a Planning Group

During preparation or pre-planning, the leader first *chooses who will be in the program planning group.* At first thought, you may say, "Well the staff will be our planning group, or, I may just plan things myself." The most effective programs are planned with a group. The energy and ideas that are created within a group are difficult to obtain when only one individual is involved. Also, when just one individual is involved, there are fewer people to delegate tasks to, so the program may not be as grand, or well-organized as it could have been.

When choosing a planning group, the leader needs to *encourage and promote youth involvement.* The ownership that comes into play when youth themselves are involved in planning is an important part of interesting them in the program or event, as well as creating opportunities for development of leadership skills and building of self-esteem. Youth will be able to offer input regarding what they *want to do.*

A third important consideration in choosing a planning group is whether or not you need to *include people with a particular type of expertise* (e.g. sports, arts, fitness) to be involved in planning, or people from other youth-serving agencies (schools, clubs) to coordinate efforts. You may also want to have representation from parents at some planning meetings so that you give them an opportunity to offer their suggestions and input.

Choosing a Planning Process

The leader *must also choose a planning process*. It is recommended that the process presented in this program guide be used. However, this process can be modified or simplified depending upon the particular needs of the youth leader. Within the planning process, the leader will need to choose meeting dates, meeting times and a location.

Whatever process is used, the basic tasks that need to be addressed are: 1) some type of needs assessment so that programs are what youth want and need; 2) setting program objectives so the youth leader understands what the program is supposed to accomplish; 3) use of a program development checklist; 4) having a strategy for effective program implementation; and 5) having a strategy for evaluating the program in terms of whether or not it accomplished what you intended it to accomplish.

Review of Prior Program Efforts

During the preparation phase, it is helpful for the leader to *review past program efforts* as found in brochures, reports and manuals, both within and outside the organization. You may want to write to other large recreation departments for brochures that describe the types of programs they offer. This can be a source of new and creative ideas.

Personal Notes:
Program Preparation:

Review the action steps that are involved in program preparation, presented in this section. Based upon past experiences and your knowledge what are some of the things that you would consider when deciding who will help you plan your program?

1. _____
2. _____
3. _____

Have you included youth themselves? Individuals with specialized knowledge or skills, if applicable? Individuals from other organizations, if applicable?

CHAPTER 11

INITIAL
PLANNING

The initial planning phase of the program planning process is perhaps the most important phase. This is because it lays the groundwork for the rest of the programming effort. This part of the process must be carried out effectively in order to provide programs that meet youth's needs. This chapter of the book offers information regarding this second step of the program planning process — initial planning, which involves: 1) finding out what youth need and want; 2) review of youth development factors that offer a base for planning; 3) encouraging youth involvement; and 4) reviewing organizational resources.

As a result of reviewing this chapter, you will be able to:

▶ Understand the value of conducting a needs assessment.

▶ Produce more effective programs and activities based on a review of youth development factors.

▶ Assess your organization's resources related to program planning and engage in entrepreneurship to augment resources.

Following is the *initial planning step* as it appears in the program planning diagram:

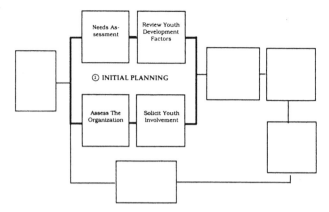

Encouraging youth involvement and leadership during this part of the planning process will increase the likelihood of success of programs, in terms of interest, commitment and attendance. The five activities carried out by the youth leader during initial planning, include:

❑   Needs assessment

❑   Review of youth development factors

❑   Assessment of the organization

❑   Soliciting youth involvement

❑   Entrepreneurship

Needs Assessment. The youth leader must find out what youth need in order to provide relevant programs and activities. It is important that the leader provide programs that youth need and not what the *leader wants.*

Review of Youth Development Factors. The youth leader must consider youth development factors in initial program planning, including youth development in terms of competencies, needs and values.

Assessment of the Organization. Prior to selecting programs, the youth leader must assess his/her organization in terms of the resources that can be used in programming, including facilities, materials, supplies and staff.

Solicit Youth Involvement. One of the most important parts of initial planning is getting youth involved. Youth should have an opportunity to help in planning, as well as opportunities for program leadership.

Entrepreneurship. The youth leader may also be able to add to existing resources by using creative strategies. Several "entrepreneurial" strategies that the leader may use to expand program opportunities at no extra cost are scrounging, collaboration, sponsorships, volunteerism and gifts/donations.

These five initial planning activities will be discussed in the following portion of this chapter.

NEEDS ASSESSMENT

Needs assessment, as the name suggests, is a process for gathering information regarding the needs and wants of youth, and then using this information to select and set priorities for program planning that meet youths' needs. Once youth needs are identified, the youth leader evaluates them in terms of the values of the organization and the degree to which it has the resources to provide the desired services.

Purpose of Needs Assessments

Needs assessment, or studying the needs of youth, is used to help with the planning and on-going evaluation of different types of programs. Following are five of the most common questions answered by a needs assessment:

What programs do people want? This question is focused on what programs youth have expressed that they want or need.

What are youths' and parents' attitudes, opinions regarding programs and services? This question deals more with youths' feelings about participating in programs, coming to the youth center, why they like/or don't like to participate in programs, and other issues. This type of information may be obtained informally, or in a more formal questionnaire or survey which may be administered to youth and/or parents.

Which groups need services? This question is focused on determining which groups are not receiving needed services. For example, in some communities there are not enough programs available for teens.

Which alternatives would be the most relevant? Your organization may have a number of requests for different types of programs and will need to determine which of the programs should be selected in terms of meeting the needs of youth to be served. In determining which programs and services to offer, decisions should not be based solely on quantitative information (e.g., potential number of participants), but on qualitative factors as well, including degree of impact for smaller groups and organizational values and vision.

What should be changed to make programs more effective? The youth leader may ask youth/parents/others how effective programs are, whether they think things should be changed or improved and, if so, how.

Sources of Information for Needs Assessments

The youth leader may use various sources to gain information regarding youth and their needs. *Youth/parent surveys* and *community surveys* often have input regarding the types of programs youth and their parents want. Some of the resources that may be useful to the leader engaged in needs assessment are listed below. ¬

❑   *Youth Needs Survey.* A youth needs survey provides information regarding the types of activities that youth currently participate in, the frequency of participation, activities that youth would like to participate in if available, as well as other questions related to youth and their problems and needs.

❑   *Community Needs Survey.* A community needs survey is a more general survey of community needs that is distributed to adults; however, it often contains a section on the needs and activities of youth. The responses of the adults to the questions about youth needs and activities are often summarized in this type of report.

❑   *Participant Evaluations.* Participant evaluations summarize how specific activities and classes are perceived by youth who have participated in them. Youths fill out this form after participation in the program. Youth services staff summarize the responses of youth and use this information for future planning.

❑   *Youth Service Organization Annual Reports.* Annual reports may also contain valuable information regarding current and eligible users of youth services. This information can also be used to help provide a basis for planning.

❑   *Youth Advisory/Planning Groups.* Information from youth advisory groups can also be useful to the leader when assessing youths' needs. If there is not a youth advisory group within your organization, you may want to develop one. This allows you to get input from youth as well as others interested in youth issues.

❑   *Informal Information Gathering.* The youth leader can obtain useful information through informal conversations and group meetings with youth, parents and others.

❑   *Other Sources of Information.* When conducting a needs assessment, the leader should also consider the programs presented by other organizations in the community, such as churches, clubs, youth-serving agencies, schools, and other groups, so that services are coordinated. In addition, suggestion programs may yield useful information.

Needs assessment is not a one-time process, but rather an ongoing process of being "tuned in" to the needs of youth. Even simply talking to youth or taking small informal surveys can offer useful information, although it will not be representative of all youth that can potentially be served by the organization. Information related to needs assessment can be used to justify new programs, based on the needs of parents and youth.

It is important to try to assess the needs of, and to reach, the youth that are *not* attending current programs and services, as well as those who are. Needs assessments also attempt to determine what problems might be preventing youth from participating in programs, such as the program location, time of day or cost. Following is a "Needs Assessment Checklist" that the leader can use to help determine program needs.

NEEDS ASSESSMENT CHECKLIST

❑   Review reports regarding youth and parents (community needs surveys, youth needs surveys, participant evaluations, and annual reports).

❑   Read about current trends related to youth. What are their impact on youth? What types of programs are indicated?

❑   Does your organization have a suggestion program? If so, find out if suggestions have been made requesting programs.

❑   Get input from youth advisory groups/youth planning groups. If one does not exist, consider starting one.

❑   Talk to youth, ask them what they want. Find out what youth do, what they watch, read, study. Do your own informal needs assessment survey of youth/parents.

REVIEW YOUTH DEVELOPMENT FACTORS

As a part of the initial planning process, the leader will find a review of the factors that relate to youth development useful. An understanding of current trends that affect youth as well as an understanding of youth competencies, the developmental stages of youth and values, is a foundation for effective programming.

✓ *Review Current Issues and Trends.* There have been many changes in the last several decades in the problems confronted by youth. A number of trends point to problems related to youth; however, there are also many youth who *do not experience severe problems.*

Some of the current national trends that might impact on programming needs are the *decline in physical health of youth, an increase in the number of youth at risk for failing school, substance abuse and delinquent behavior, a dramatic increase in the number of youth needing out-of-school care, an increase in diversity, declining resources and greater mobility.*

✓ *Consider Youth Development Competencies/Needs.* Basic youth development objectives or *competencies* have been developed that are important for youth to attain in order to become positive, healthy adults. The five competencies, as adapted from Pittman and Write (1991), include: *Health and physical competence, personal and social competence, cognitive and creative competence, vocational competence and citizenship and ethics competencies.* As youth move toward mastering these areas, they also progress in their feelings of achievement and self esteem. Youth need to be good at something in order to feel good about themselves.

✓ *Consider Developmental Stages of Youth.* In order to successfully plan and implement effective and relevant programs, an understanding is needed by the leader of the qualities that characterize youth of different ages. With this knowledge, the leader can choose programs and activities that respond to, and correspond to, the developmental stages of the individuals for whom he/she is programming.

The chapter of the book devoted to youth development presents information regarding the different developmental stages of youth. It is broken down by age categories, including 6-9 year olds, 10-12 year olds, 13-15 year olds, and 16 to 18 year olds.

✓   *Identify Targeted Values.* Values are *principles or guidelines that individuals believe to be important in life.* Youth leaders, both intentionally and unintentionally, transmit values to youth. It is important for youth leaders to be aware of the way in which they impact upon the values of youth.

Some of the values that the leader may want to emphasize are independence, responsibility, leadership, respect for others, trust, industriousness and teamwork. Very often, values determine the course of action that an individual will take, and will influence the way in which they direct their energy.

Youth - Centered Programming

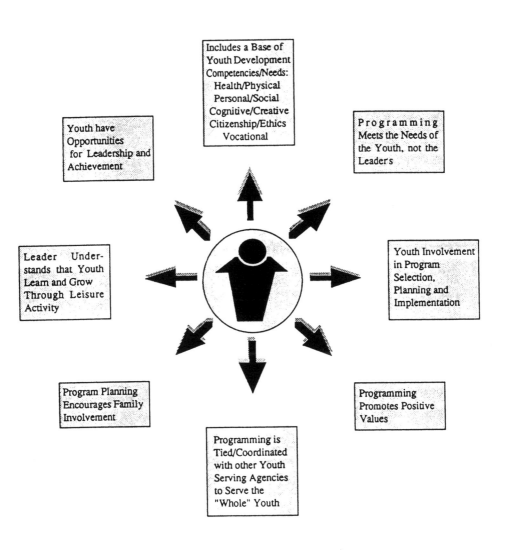

ASSESSMENT OF YOUR
ORGANIZATION'S RESOURCES

Prior to program development and during the initial phase of planning, the leader must determine what resources are available for programs and activities. This will determine the support that is available for programs. Following is a checklist that can be used to consider organizational resources and to connect with other organizations in order to maximize effectiveness.

❑   List the open spaces, playing fields, rooms, gyms, pools, and other areas and facilities you have within your organization.

❑   List the types of supplies you have. What is available to you? How can you use them?

❑   List the equipment that is available to you. What can you get on loan from other organizations? How can you use this?

❑   Find out what is available that you could use commercially by assessing youth a fee/charge (theme parks, bowling alleys, skating rinks, miniature golf, cultural sites).

❑   Find out what is available from public organizations or non-profit organizations. What about schools? From other youth-serving organizations?

❑   Find out what might be available from area businesses. For example, is sponsorship of one of your activities available? Food? Equipment? Uniforms? Businesses often sponsor events as a part of their public relations.

❑   What staff do you have available? Can you call on others to help you — parents, volunteers, community clubs, youth themselves?

❏   How can you coordinate with other agencies/ groups to expand your programs?

SOLICIT YOUTH INVOLVEMENT/LEADERSHIP

All youth within programs should have available opportunities for meaningful, "real" leadership. Youth are often undervalued. Youth should be included, not only in initial planning and organization, but should have opportunities to organize their own programs and activities. Youth involvement/leadership can be solicited through youth advisory groups, youth planning groups and youth representation within the organization's planning group.

If youth advisory/planning groups do not exist for your organization, you may want to help develop such a group to offer input. Youth may be involved in selecting activities, as well as developing a strategy for carrying them out, including facilities, roles and responsibilities, equipment, materials, outline or schedule of events, publicity, systems for control, anticipated outcomes, time and date of program, step-by-step visualization of the event, and other relevant activities.

ENTREPRENEURSHIP

The youth leader may also be able to add to existing resources by using creative strategies. Following are several "entrepreneurial" strategies that the leader may use to expand program opportunities at no extra cost.

❏   **Scrounging.** In addition to using existing resources, the youth leader may brainstorm ideas for "scrounging" materials and services. To be successful, all programmers must be good at scrounging. Scrounging involves the recycling of "free" materials for use in programs and activities. Cans, potato chip containers, paper tubes, refrigerator boxes, and other items can be collected by kids and staff and used in program activities. The leader can also create an "Opportunity Box" of scraps at the center, and let kids use things out of it to invent and create.

❑   **Collaboration/Cooperation.** The youth leader may be able to find other organizations that are willing to cooperate and/or collaborate to offer youth services. A youth service organization might enter into a partnership with another organization, such as a school, to share resources to produce programs and activities that are mutually beneficial. Partnerships can be formed between departments within governmental units, or with other organizations.

❑   **Sponsorships.** There are a number of different ways to encourage community groups, fraternal organizations and businesses to provide sponsorships of youth services. Sponsors usually offer financial support in exchange for advertising or publicity rights in conjunction with an event.

❑   **Involvement of Constituents.** The youth leader may involve youth themselves in fund-raising projects, to earn money for trips, materials and other items. A car wash, "fun run," can drive, bake sale and other events can accomplish this purpose, as well as giving youth a sense of involvement, independence and achievement.

❑   **Gifts and Donations.** A gift or donation from an individual or business is an outright contribution in support of the work of an organization. Gifts can come in the form of equipment, supplies or other items; they do not necessarily have to be a cash contribution.

Adding Programs and Activities Without Additional Cost Through Entrepreneurship

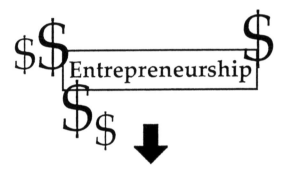

Use of the Media

Collaboration/Cooperation With Other Organizations

Sponsorships

Reciprocation

Scrounging

Innovation/Creativity

Involvement of Constituents

Edginton, Christopher Edginton, Reprint by Permission

A Final Note

In the initial planning stage, fact finding is a critical element. Initial planning involves finding out what youth want, what their needs are, and what kinds of developmental factors may be addressed in the program planning process. The resources necessary to implement programs must be linked with needs in order to produce services that are developmentally sound. Thorough initial planning will increase the likelihood that subsequent steps in the program planning process will proceed more smoothly.

Personal Notes:
Initial Planning

What are things you can do to make your programs youth centered?

_____
_____
_____
_____
_____

What do the terms youth leadership and youth involvement mean in terms of program planning?

_____
_____
_____
_____

What are the five questions answered by a needs assessment?

_____
_____
_____
_____

What sources/surveys are available to you to help with needs assessment?

_____

_____

_____

_____

_____

References

Pittman, K.J. and M. Wright (1991). *A Rationale for Enhancing the Role of the Non-School Voluntary Sector in Youth Development.* New York: Center for Youth Development and Policy Research.

CHAPTER 12

PROGRAM OBJECTIVES

As a youth leader, you will be responsible for providing direction to program services. This section of the book offers information regarding the third step of the program planning process — identifying program objectives. It is goals and objectives that drive the work of the organization and move it forward in a coordinated and effective manner.

What is it that the youth leader wants to accomplish through implementation of programs and services? What is the purpose of the program or activity? It is important that the leader consider program goals and objectives during the planning process.

As a result of reading this chapter you will be able to :

▶ Establish direction for program services by selecting goals and objectives.

▶ Increase the impact of programs by using guidelines to write effective performance learning objectives.

▶ Gain knowledge of three domains of learning.

Following is the step of the program plan that involves *identifying program objectives.*

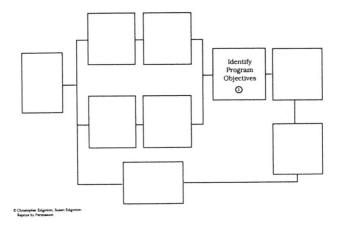

It is this step in the process—identifying program objectives—that enables the leader to link program goals with youth development needs. In this chapter, the following will be presented.

☐   Selecting general program goals and objectives

☐   Developing performance/learning objectives for youth

☐   Using information regarding domains of learning

☐   Using guidelines for writing performance/learning objectives

Types of Program Goals and Objectives

Establishing program goals has two important results: 1) It allows the leader to measure whether or not the goals were achieved, and thereby measure performance; and 2) it allows the leader to operate effectively and efficiently, by planning in advance. Program goals are usually related to:

☐   **Program Development.** Program development goals and objectives focus on such questions as: What will be the content of the program? What are the underlying youth development competencies that will be addressed? Where will the program be located? Who will the participants be, what ages? What are the considerations regarding cost and fees?

❑   **Promotion.** Goals and objectives related to promotion and advertising focus on such questions as: What type of promotion will be used — flyers, brochures, television, newspapers, other? Who are we trying to reach, and how can we best get the word to them? When should the information be distributed?

❑   **Financial Considerations.** Goals and objectives related to financial considerations focus on such questions as: Should we charge a fee? What is the break-even point for the program? Will the organization subsidize this program and if so, to what degree? How is money going to be handled by staff? Will fees be charged and if so, can all youth afford them?

PERFORMANCE/LEARNING OBJECTIVES FOR YOUTH

In addition to general program goals, the youth leader must decide what behavior youth will exhibit or demonstrate as a result of participation in the program — what is it that youth/ learners can do at the end of a program, and how will you know that they have done it?

Whatever it is that you want youth to accomplish as a result of participating in your program, you must write out objectives in a very specific way following certain guidelines. This is done so that you may later evaluate whether the objectives you set have been achieved.

It is important that the youth leader and the participant have the same goal and that it is clear. For example:

> ... Each youth in the group will demonstrate that they know the sequence and form of the game "Giants, Wizards and Elves," by playing it in a line formation in which each youth leads once.

General Guidelines for Writing Performance/ Learning Objectives

Program goals and objectives must be written in a particular way in order to be effective. Following is a guideline or checklist for writing program objectives, as adapted from Edginton, Hanson & Edginton (1992). When writing goals and objectives, they must be:

✓   *Specific.* Program objectives are clear and specific.

✓   *Measurable.* In order to be able to determine that the desired behavior or results have been achieved, objectives must be measurable. There must be a way to "count" the result.

✓   *Reality-based.* Program objectives must be realistic and attainable.

✓   *Useful.* Program objectives must be of value to the leader and the participants, and they must be used.

✓   *Linked to Youth Needs.* Most importantly, program objectives must be linked to the developmental competencies and needs of youth as outlined in this program training guide.

Well-written program goals and objectives not only provide a structure for planning, but they provide direction for the efforts of the youth leader. The structure of program goals and objectives can be simple or complicated; youth leaders writing them for the first time often make them too complicated.

Stating Objectives in Terms of the Leader's Actions

The leader writing a performance objective will attempt to describe the performance that he/she wants youth to be able to demonstrate or exhibit before they will be considered competent.

PROGRAM OBJECTIVES SHOULD
ANSWER THESE QUESTIONS

WHO   Who will demonstrate
                               the outcome

CONDITIONS   Conditions under which
                                      the behavioral out-
                                      come will be exhibited

WHAT   What behavior is expected

LEVEL   Level of
                                 acceptable performance

The leader and the participant (youth) should have a clear, and similar understanding of the goal of the program, as well as clear criteria on which to base an evaluation of the youth's progress. One of the ways that objectives can be stated is in terms of the leader's actions. For example:

> To demonstrate Giants, Elves, Wizards.
> To lead the group in singing The Penny Song.
> To teach "cartoon drawing."

Although this defines the role of the leader, it still does not focus on the participant (youth) and what he/she will accomplish. It also does not give an indication of the degree of learning that is to take place, nor the quality.

Stating Objectives in Terms of the Participant's Actions

Objectives should also describe the behavior to be exhibited by the participant (youth), showing that the youth has learned or mastered the activity. A performance or learning objective stated from the participant's (youth's) view, would read as follows.

> Each participant in the group, having been shown a demonstration of The Penny Song, will demonstrate that he/she knows the words to the song by singing it through twice with the group, as observed by the leader, without mistakes.

Some objectives also have a time element, and other criteria for measurement. Following is a simple guideline for writing objectives. There are other methods that can be used as well, this is just one approach.

❏   Say what is going to be accomplished. This is the action the youth will eventually demonstrate — for example, "To hit the ball."

❏   Say how you will measure the objective to determine that it has been accomplished. "The ball will make contact with the bat and move forward within the playing field."

❏   Give the minimum level of acceptable achievement of the objective. "The youth will hit the ball 5 out of 10 times that it is pitched to him/her and it is within striking range."

Again, it is important to have an understanding, particularly in skill development, of the outcomes desired as well as the behaviors that will need to be demonstrated in order to determine that the desired outcomes have been achieved.

What are the Behaviors You Want to Develop?

Before writing behavioral or performance objectives, you must decide *what behaviors* you want youth to develop or change. Do you want youth to develop certain physical skills? If so, which physical skills? Or, do you want them to develop other types of skills?

It is helpful at this point for the leader to have information regarding the types of learning behaviors in which youth may engage. A set of three "taxonomies" are available that outline types of behaviors by category, including "thinking, feeling and action" behaviors. These charts represent an effective starting point for writing performance objectives.   A more specific discussion of these follows in this portion of the chapter.

DOMAINS OF LEARNING

Learning Taxonomies have been developed by Bloom (1956) Krathwohl (1964) and Bush (1972). These taxonomies identify different levels of learning within the cognitive, affective and psychomotor domains. Following is further definition of these domains. This information is useful to the youth leader when deciding upon and writing performance objectives.

Cognitive Domain

Cognitive development is related to those processes by which youth think, know and gain an awareness of objects and events. Following is a chart of the major categories in the Cognitive Domain of development. The simplest form of learning is at the top of the table. *As youth progress from one level to the next, they have experienced growth.*

COGNITIVE DOMAIN
Major Categories in the Cognitive Domain
1. Knowledge—Knowledge is defined as the remembering of previously learned material.
2. Comprehension—Comprehension is defined as the ability to grasp the meaning of material.
3. Application—Application refers to the ability to use learned material in new and concrete situations.
4. Analysis—Analysis refers to the ability to break down material into its component parts so that its organizational structure may be understood.
5. Synthesis—Synthesis refers to the ability to put parts together to form a new whole.
6. Evaluation—Evaluation is concerned with the ability to judge the value of material for a given purpose.

Bloom 1956

In terms of cognitive development, the youth leader will need to determine whether the learner will (1) merely possess the knowledge, (2) understand it, (3) analyze it, (4) apply it, (5) synthesize it with other knowledge, or (6) evaluate it.

Psychomotor/Physical Development

The Psychomotor Domain of development includes the acquisition of physical and neuromuscular skills. In terms of psychomotor skills, youth progress from imitation, to manipulation, to precision, to articulation and naturalization. The Psychomotor Domain is the skill domain involving movement. The acts of playing ball, writing and speaking are examples of learning in this domain.

Following is a chart of the major categories in the Psychomotor Domain of development (Bush, 1972). The simplest form of learning is at the top of the table. *As youth progress from one level to the next, they have experienced growth and learning.*

PSYCHOMOTOR DOMAIN

Major Categories in the Psychomotor Domain

1. Imitation—imitation of some observed act usually lacking neuro-muscular coordination.

2. Manipulation—Manipulation emphasizes skill in following directions.

3. Precision—Precision emphasizes accuracy, exactness, and control with reduction of errors.

4. Articulation—Articulation involves coordination of a series of acts—involves accuracy and control, plus elements of speed and time.

5. Naturalization—Naturalization occurs when the act has become routine, automatic, and spontaneous. Performance is natural and smooth.

Bush 1972

Affective Development

The Affective Domain of development involves feelings, values and emotions. The Affective Domain of learning may involve an attitudinal change, an appreciation or the development of an interest. In terms of the Affective Domain, learners may (1) merely receive or become aware of the existence of an attitude; (2) respond as a result of that awareness; (3) value the particular attitude, interest or appreciation; (4) organize the attitude or interest into a value system; or (5) internalize the attitude, interest or appreciation so that it becomes a positive characteristic of behavior.

Following is a chart of the major categories in the Affective Domain. The simplest form of learning is at the top of the table. *As youth progress from one level to the next, they have experienced growth and learning.*

AFFECTIVE DOMAIN

Major Categories in the Affective Domain

1. Receiving—Receiving refers to the client's willingness to attend to particular phenomena or stimuli.

2. Responding—Responding refers to active participation on the part of the participant.

3. Valuing—Valuing is concerned with the work or value a client attaches to a particular object, phenomenon, or behavior.

4. Organization—Organization is concerned with bringing together different values, resolving conflicts between them, and beginning the building of an internally consistent value system.

5. Characterization by a Value or Value Complex—At this level of the affective domain, the individual has a value system that has controlled his behavior for a sufficiently long enough time for him to have developed a characteristic "lifestyle."

Krathwohl 1964

Linking Program Goals to Youth Development/Needs. Youth development principles, ages/stages of youth development, youth development competencies and basic needs of youth are discussed within the youth development chapter of the book. These factors should be considered and included when the leader is developing program goals and objectives.

Three Aspects of Healthy Youth

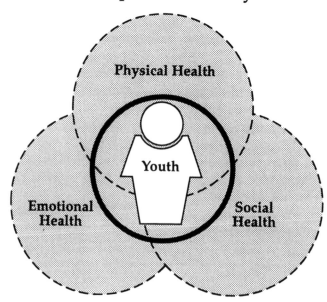

A Final Note

Program objectives provide direction to the youth leader's program planning efforts. The development of program objectives, requires the leader to consider the potential impact and opportunities provided by youth programs and activities and, then, to use this information to meet the individual-specific needs of youth. It also allows the leader to track the progress of youth, as a group and individually, and to measure the degree to which they have grown and developed over time.

Personal Notes: Identifying Program Objectives

Why is it important to identify program objectives?

_____

_____

_____

What are characteristics of program objectives?

_____

_____

_____

Identify program objectives for a child engaged in the game Giants, Wizards and Elves.

_____

_____

_____

References

Bloom, B.S. (1956). *Taxonomy of Educational Objectives: Cognitive Domain*. New York: McKay.

Bush, P. (1972). *A Program Course for Writing of Performance Objectives*.Chico,CA: North California Program Development Center.

Krathwohl, D.R. (1964). *Taxonomy of Educational Objectives: Affective Domain*. New York: McKay.

Edginton, C.R., C.J. Hanson and S.R. Edginton. (1992). *Leisure Programming: Concepts, Trends and Professional Practice*. Dubuque, IA: Brown and Benchmark.

CHAPTER 13

PROGRAM
DEVELOPMENT

How does a youth leader determine which programs, activities, and events to offer youth? Does the leader offer what has been done successfully before? Or offer new activities? There are a number of methods that can be used by youth leaders to develop programs that are effective, well organized, and well-managed. Program development involves selection of the program area, specific program and program format, organization of program tasks and program promotion.

As a result of reviewing this chapter you will be able to:

▶ Gain an understanding of seven approaches to program development as well as different program formats that you can use in programming, including competitive, drop-in, class, club, special event, and outreach.

▶ Increase the impact of programs by using activities within specific content areas, such as active games, arts and crafts, drama, nature, new games, songs, sports and others.

▶ Learn how to use a Total Quality Planning checklist and a planning and promotions checklist.

Following is the *program development* step of the planning model as it appears in the diagram.

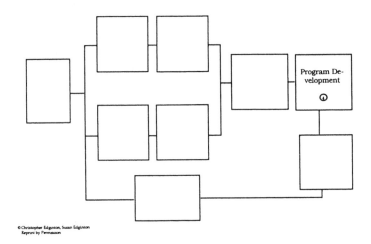

Program De-
velopment

①

It is important at this step of the process to select a balance of activities and programs from among physical activities, arts and crafts, songs, drama, and others. Following are the subjects discussed in this chapter of the book.

❑   Determining an approach(es) to program development

❑   Selecting a program format

❑   Selecting the program area

❑   Using a program development checklist

❑   Implementing a plan for program promotion—publicity, advertising.

Program development is the fourth step in the program planning process. It is at this stage, that the youth leader is involved in selecting the program and program format, as well as managing the details that must be accomplished in order to implement the program.
Following is a discussion of the first of these topics— Approaches to Program Development.

APPROACHES TO PROGRAM DEVELOPMENT

During the *program development* phase of program planning, the leader must decide what programs will be provided, in what type of format and with what resources. Following are six (6) approaches for developing programs, (Edginton, Hansen & Edginton 1992).

- ❑ Traditional Approach
- ❑ Current Practice Approach
- ❑ Expressed Desires Approach
- ❑ Cafeteria Approach
- ❑ Prescriptive Approach
- ❑ Objectives Approach
- ❑ Combined Approach

Traditional Approach. The leader depends on what has been done in past years for program ideas.

Current Practice Approach. The leader follows the latest trends as a basis for program ideas, as well as what is going on in other organizations currently.

Expressed Desires Approach. This approach involves use of surveys and other similar material as a basis for program planning.

Cafeteria Approach. The leader using this approach offers several different programs and services, and lets youth pick from among them.

Prescriptive Approach. This approach is most commonly used in the therapeutic recreation setting, often to respond to dysfunctional behavior.

Objectives Approach. The leader using this approach sets performance and/or learning objectives that specify outcomes expected from program participation.

Combined Approach. As the name suggests, this approach recommends using any one or more of the above approaches depending on the circumstances.

These approaches are discussed in more detail in the following section.

Traditional Approach to Programming

Probably the most commonly used method of program development is the *traditional approach*, which *depends on information about what has been done before within the organization* in order to plan for the future. A youth leader who uses the traditional approach would look back at old brochures, schedules, activity guides and use this information to produce a program for the current year. Is this approach a good one?

What are The Benefits of This Approach?

- The traditional approach to planning programs is *less work*. The youth leader uses what has been done before, rather than generating new ideas.

- It is *a safe approach* — programs that have worked in the past, may be more likely to be successful in the future.

- The *expectations of youth are consistent* with what is offered by the organization — they expect the same thing every year, and they get it.

What are the Problems with This Approach?

- Traditional programs and activities have their place in the mix of programs offered, but exclusive use of them is *uninspiring* — how can you expect youth to get excited about the same programs every year?

- It also may be difficult for *the youth leader* to be enthused about programs and activities that are "old news" and are not dynamic and new.

- This method doesn't take into account the fact that *people change, situations change, facilities change, youths' interests change, current events change and fads change.* Programs selected this way *may not be current, contemporary, fresh, innovative.*

Recommendations. Good youth leaders strive to be fresh, creative innovative, current and dynamic. It is not possible to use only the traditional approach to programming and achieve these goals. *The best youth leaders strive to make each year's activities **better** than those of previous years.*

Current Practice Approach to Program Development

A *current practice approach* to programming relies heavily on adopting program strategies and plans that are current trends and that are being used widely by other communities or youth program leaders. The youth leader using this approach identifies and copies current trends and the current programs of other communities or program leaders, as gathered from brochures, professional magazines and professional meetings.

What are the Benefits of This Approach?

- Looking at current trends in other communities *can give the youth leader new ideas* regarding types of programs that interest youth today.

- Programs that have been offered in other communities will have already been *tested and found to be successful*, and the youth leader can take advantage of their experience.

- The current practice approach offers an *easy way to sell programming plans and strategies to the community and staff* —"if it's a popular programming trend elsewhere, then it will surely work for us."

What are the Problems with This Approach?

• As a leader it is important to make a connection with current trends and fads. However, the fact remains that *just because an activity flourishes in one community does not assure that it will be of equal popularity in your community.*

• The current practices approach *ignores the fact that each community and youth population is unique,* with a separate set of needs and values, different resources, and a wide range of cultural diversity. This approach *builds programs around what is "in" instead of the actual interests.*

Recommendations. Although as a youth leader you should "stay in tune" with current trends and fads in other communities and consider them as program options, you should also *test these types of ideas with your youth and community.* Have you observed or talked with local youth and parents recently? Have you spent time getting to know their needs and values? Or, have you assumed that you know what they want and what is in their minds?

Expressed Desires Approach to Program Development

The youth leader using the *expressed desires* approach to programming uses surveys, interviews or interest checklists to allow youth to "express" what types of programs they desire and the activities in which they would like to participate. The youth leader then uses this information to plan and offer programs that youth say that they want and would attend.

What are the Benefits of This Approach?

• This approach allows *youth to have input into the types of programs, activities and events* that are chosen by the youth leader.

• This approach not only gives the youth leader information about what youth desire, it also *has the effect of generating interest by youth in programs,* activities and events. Youth will be more interested in programs in which they have expressed an interest.

• The youth leader using this approach may be *less likely to experience program failures, and spend time, effort, and resources to plan programs and activities that may not be desired* by community youth and parents.

What are the Problems with This Approach?

• Although the "expressed desires" approach may sound like an ideal solution to selecting programs, *youth often do not express what they really want to do,* but rather what they think their friends would say or what they think the youth leader wants them to say. The information they provide may or may not be a reflection of their actual feelings.

• Second, *youth have limited experience* and, as a result, their input is also limited by their previous experiences. There may be programs that they would enjoy, but if they don't know about them or understand them they will not select them as being desired.

Recommendations. The "expressed desires" approach, using surveys and questionnaires to gain input from youth, is *an effective tool in planning programs, but should not be used as the sole basis for selecting programs.* Although the youth leader should not make program assumptions without input from youth, the input received should not be the only basis for selection of programs.

Prescriptive Approach to Program Development

Participation in leisure programs and activities has the power to ultimately affect social and personal outcomes. Play is powerful, and the way in which the youth leader uses the power of play can determine positive or negative outcomes.

The "prescriptive approach" is usually used in the therapeutic recreation setting; however, it can be used in any leisure service. The youth leader using this approach, attempts to *intervene with programs to meet social, physical, and other needs of youth.* The youth leader typically uses this approach with youth who exhibit dysfunctional behavior.

What are the Benefits of This Approach?

*   This approach is *individually designed to meet the needs of youth* who show signs of social symptoms that need attention. It is a very specific form of program planning that has therapeutic benefits.

*   Use of this approach by the youth leader has *the effect of encouraging the leader to focus on the needs of youth,* rather than on program details, and to view youth "holistically," in terms of his/her needs as a person.

What are the Problems with This Approach?

*   This approach is *time consuming,* both in terms of initial planning and in individual attention as the specialized program plan is carried out.

*   This approach is constructive, but it is still "imposed" on the youth by the youth leader — it is *important that intervention is provided according to the needs of the participant and not the desires of the leader.*

Recommendations. The "prescriptive approach" to programming has a place in program planning *if the youth leader has the knowledge, experience and skills* to use this approach. It is an approach that has the potential to help youth move from a dysfunctional state to a functional one within the leisure setting. Play and leisure time activities are very powerful tools that can be used to help youth develop.

Cafeteria Approach to Program Development

The cafeteria approach establishes a wide variety of program opportunities that allows youth to choose from among these programs. The youth leader using this approach emphasizes freedom of choice. The "cafeteria approach" not only offers a variety of different types of activities, but also may offer a variety of program formats. For example, activities at an ice rink could include beginning ice hockey, figure skating, free skating, stunt skating and hockey leagues.

What are the Benefits of This Approach?

- Youth often feel that they do not have influence or control in their lives. At school and at home their expected behavior and their routine is often structured and limiting. Having *freedom and flexibility within the recreation setting is very appealing to youth.*

- This approach *allows the youth leader to offer a wide range of activities to "test" appeal.* With this approach, there is a greater chance that youth will find something in which they are interested.

- The youth leader using this approach is able to offer a number of activities and eliminate the ones for which there is no interest. In this way, the youth leader is *able to avoid commitment of time and expense to conduct activities for which there is little interest in participation.*

What are the Problems with This Approach?

- One difficulty with this approach is the amount of *time and resources invested in planning what might become wasted programming* efforts.

- This approach *works well with some types of program options, but not as well with others.* It is most successfully used with classes, lessons, clubs, workshops, and other educational activities.

Recommendations. The "cafeteria approach" to programming *empowers youth to have influence over their program choices.* This is a desirable consequence, but must be balanced with available human and material resources needed to carry out additional program offerings.

Objectives Approach to Program Development

Establishing goals and objectives ties together the actions of the youth leader and the nature of programs and activities with broader goals related to the development of youth. An objectives approach allows the leader to know exactly what the underlying developmental accomplishments should be demonstrated by youth at the end of a program or activity; whether it's to throw a ball for more accuracy, or to exhibit a higher level of leadership.

What Are The Benefits Of This Approach?

- Use of the "objectives approach" *encourages the youth leader to include developmental components within program efforts* related to physical, social, emotional and psychological growth of youth.

- Measurable objectives, related to social, physical, psychological, and emotional growth, *allow the leader to determine whether programs and activities have helped youth develop* and to what degree.

- This approach *encourages the youth leader to visualize the activity process* and determine the benefits it might produce for youth.

What are the Problems with This Approach?

- The *youth leader must have the skills and knowledge to write effective performance objectives.* Performance objectives should be specific, measurable, reality-based, useful and linked to needs.

- The youth leader can *only measure what is observable*. It can be difficult to measure changes in behaviors.

- The youth *leader needs to have knowledge of the needs of youth* in order to develop effective performance objectives.

- Developing and writing performance objectives *will take more time* and effort on the part of the youth leader.

Recommendations. *When the youth leader uses well-defined program objectives, it provides direction that encourages youth development.* It allows the youth leader to bridge the gap between means and ends. Specific instructions for writing program objectives are covered in Chapter 12.

Combined Approach to Program Development

The final method for the development of program services is the "combined approach." With this approach, the youth leader *gathers information from a number of sources* to be used in development of program options. The youth leader using this approach uses the traditional, current practices, expressed desires, prescriptive, cafeteria, and objectives approaches to gain a broad view of program options, youth interests and youth needs.

What are the Benefits of This Approach?

- The combined approach *recognizes that the most effective approach to the development of programs may vary with the situation, youth needs and other factors.* It encourages use of the strategy or strategies that are most appropriate given the organization's needs and goals.

- This approach *allows the youth leader to gather information from a number of different sources,* including past program offerings, currently popular programs in other communities, youth needs assessments, youth development criteria, as well as others.

What are the Problems with This Approach?

- The combined approach *requires the youth leader to research a large amount of information.* It also *requires that the youth leader have the ability to evaluate the information* and make a judgment on what will meet the needs of youth.

- This approach *is more time consuming* than other, simpler, approaches, such as the traditional approach based on what was done in the past.

Recommendations. Few youth leaders rely on just one approach in the development of programs. The combined approach, using information from a number of sources to make program planning decisions, is the most effective method for planning and programming comprehensive, contemporary and effective services for youth.

Each of the methods for development of program services has merit in the program planning picture. Although it is common practice to rely heavily on the traditional approach, better programs and services will result from a combined approach to the development of program services.

SELECTING A PROGRAM FORMAT

There are various ways that the youth leader can offer and arrange programs and services for youth. These are often called *"program formats."* For example, the leader may want to involve youth in basketball, but there are many different ways to do this. What approach should be used? A league? Instructional basketball clinics to promote learning and skill development? Basketball camps? Other means? The leader can also use organizational formats such as clubs, retreats, family participation and instructional videos.

It is up to you to choose the format that will best meet the needs of your youth. *If youth are inexperienced in an activity that involves a level of complexity, you may want to begin with a type of instructional format, in order to help them build skills.* The idea behind this approach, is that the youth may enjoy the activity more later if they have a foundation of information and skills. This approach will also promote a "leveling" effect, that brings the less skilled youth up to the level of the more experienced youth, so that they can all participate with a feeling of accomplishment and self-esteem.

Types of Program Formats

Following are a number of types of program formats that can be used by the youth leader.

❑   *Competitive.* Many activities may be competitive in nature. Leagues, tournaments and contests are all types of competitive organization.

❑   *Drop-in/Open.* Using a drop-in format for programs gives kids a sense of freedom. Activities in this format are organized so that they can be ongoing, self-directed or spontaneous. Kids drop-in when they want to, and become involved in activities at will.

❑   *Class.* Instructional classes, a formal type of format, offers youth an opportunity for skill development in a certain area.

❑   *Club.* A club is a format designed for a group with a special interest. Clubs are a big hit with kids, because they can choose things they are interested in, and they have a sense of perceived freedom.

A highly successful program format is to offer youth a choice of three or four clubs to belong to each week, having each club working on different projects, which end with a demonstration on Friday. Kids can come in and work on their club projects independently with the leader acting as a resource person and coach. They have opportunity for self-direction and recognition.

❑   *Special Events.* A special event is a one-time program of large scale, such as parades, festivals,
carnivals.

❑   *Outreach.* Outreach programs attempt to go out
and serve youth in their own locale. It involves
taking the activity to the participant, rather than
the participant coming to the activity.

Before selecting a program format you, as a program leader,
must determine what activity or activities you plan to offer and
their goals and objectives. In addition, you must determine the
type of atmosphere you are trying to create — are you attempting
to promote a social situation, a learning situation, competitive
situation, or something else?

Types of Program Formats

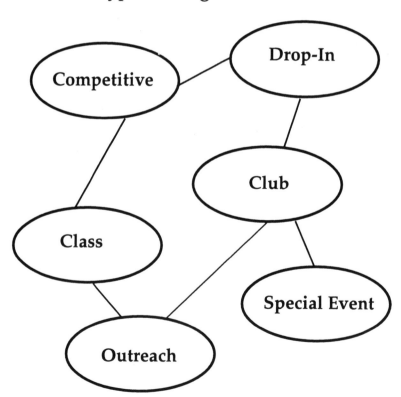

PROGRAM AREAS

The leader should have a system in place for planning out, in writing, and in advance, the activities that will be implemented during programs. In this chapter, the idea of programming using activity clusters will be discussed, as well as a sample summer day camp program and specific types of activities that can be included within programs.

Activity Clusters and Youth Development

The youth leader may tie programming to the principles of youth development. By selecting activities from each of five activity areas the youth leader will offer a balance of different types of activities that address different youth needs. Following are five activity areas from which the leader may select daily activities.

- ❑ Arts/Crafts/Drama

- ❑ Physical/Sports/Games

- ❑ Social/Leadership/Meaningfulness

- ❑ Scientific/Outdoor/World

- ❑ Values/Citizenship/Vocation

A brief discussion of each of these activity clusters follows:

✓ **Arts/Crafts/Drama.** This category of activities supports the development of youth competency in several areas, including the area of *cognitive/ creative* skills. Not only do youth have a need to be creative, but this type of activity gives kids something tangible that they have made or done that they can point to. Imaginative activities and play during childhood contribute the ability to think abstractly and conceptually, which are important later in life. In addition, some arts and crafts can help youth build an interest in activities that will become life skills.

✓   **Physical/Sports/Games.** This category of activities supports the development of youth competency in a number of areas, including the area of *health/physical* skills. This type of activity helps youth develop life-long skills that will ensure their current and future health and fitness. Learning about teamwork, fair play, "everybody wins," and the importance of fitness are all part of this category of activity.

✓   **Social/Leadership/Meaningfulness.** Activities within this area help youth develop skills related to *personal/social* competence. An important component of these types of activities is the concept of meaningfulness; that is activities that help people bond meaningfully together by doing something for others, talking about issues, feelings and values, engaging in traditions, singing quiet songs, learning new things, and other activities. Also included in this area is leadership; that is offering all youth opportunities for leadership and planning, assuming responsibility and making decisions.

✓   **Scientific/Outdoor/World.** This category of activities supports the development of youth competency in several areas, including the area of *cognitive/creative* skills. Problem-solving, analytical skills, interest in learning and achieving are all skills that can be cultivated within this program area. In addition, values related to exploration, harmony between people and preserving our environment can be built into these types of activities.

✓   **Values/Citizenship/Vocation.** This category of activities supports the development of youth competency in the areas of *vocation* and *citizenship* as well as other areas. Helping youth build a desire to contribute to nation and community is an important component of leisure service organizations.

Youth programs also may offer an opportunity to inform youth about different future vocational or job opportunities, by having individuals come to the youth center and tell about their jobs, or by having youth go on field trips to other organizations. *More than 80% of jobs in the future will be in the service sector of employment* so knowledge about these types of job opportunities will be important to youth.

Bag of Tricks

Youth leaders will need to develop a "bag of tricks" to be used during lulls in programs, and when something unexpected happens and leaves the leader with plenty of kids, but no activity. The leader should put together a "kit" of games, songs, puzzles, riddles, jokes, magic tricks, crafts and activity cards, that he/she can use on the spur of the moment.

SPECIFIC CONTENT AREAS

This section offers specific content areas that youth leaders can incorporate into their programs. By using a number of program formats and content areas, the youth leader is able to offer a variety of programs that will meet various needs of youth.

Activities for content areas may be organized on 5" x 7" note cards by the youth leader and stored in a resource file. It is recommended that youth leaders develop and/or purchase a resource file of games, songs, arts and crafts, special events and other activities. This not only presents content areas, but offers an example of a resource card for each type of content area.

In the content areas listed below, as adapted from DeGraaf and DeGraaf (1994) the reader may notice that there is some overlap; this is to be expected as in most program resources activities are often cross referenced to avoid confusion. For example, an activity such as "pine cone bird feeders" is a craft, but it could also be classified as a nature activity. Codes used in this section include the following: Cooperative activities (C); Icebreakers and introductory games (I); Nature activities (N); Action songs (A); Quiet songs (Q); and Rounds (R); Bus activities (B); Water activities (W); Brainteasers (T); and Special Events (SE). The following content areas will be presented here, with a sample activity card for each area.

• Active Games
• Aquatics
• Crafts
• Drama
• Initiative Games
• Low Organized Games

• Music
• Nature
• New Games
• Rainy Day
• Special Events
• Sports

Following is a discussion of each of these areas.

Active Games. Active games are generally characterized by those games and sports which require a large, open area and high energy (i.e. tag games, new games) If you're playing these games correctly, you ought to feel some sweat on your brow! Active games are usually played in large areas because of the amount of space needed and the larger number of participants required.

Types of Active Games:

Action Scavenger Hunt	Back Ball Relay	Balloon Basketball
Balloon Pop Relay	Balloon Soccer	Barnyard
Charades	Egg Race	Elephant, Rhino, Rabbit
Fire in the Mountain	Frisbee Golf	Human Bingo
Indoor Scavenger Hunt	Killer	Link Tag
Miniature Bowling	Musical Hats	Nerf Baseball
Shoe Kick	Snake	Squirrel in a Tree
Steal the Bacon	Three-Legged Race	Triangle and One
Typhoon	Who's Missing	Why and Because
Hoop Tag	Jet Pilot	Parachute Game
Poison Ball	Twistin' Relay	Two Deep

Aquatics. Aquatic activities provide structured fun during swimming times and are often designed to improve specific swimming skills. Thus, youth are able to "practice" particular techniques without experiencing the drudgery of a routine workout. Songs with movement, as well as games, can be incorporated into swimming time and should reflect the program theme. An example might be:

Alligator Tag

Group Size	3-30	**Ages**	5 and up
Equipment	None	**Pool**	Deep
Objective	To tag all others and make them "alligators"	**Code**	W

Directions	Set up boundaries. One person is the alligator and tries to tag the other players, turning them into alligators, who also help tag. To avoid being tagged, players can float on their backs with their knees up out of the water. They are safe from the alligator as long as they hold this position.
Rules	Swimming ability is required.
Safety	Standard Safety Procedures.
Theme	In their travels youth have entered an alligator-infested swamp and safety can only be found if youth can impersonate the alligators.

Types of Aquatic Activities:

Ball Tag	Belly Flop Contest	Biggest Splash
Bucket Relay	Crows and Cranes	Disrobing Relay
Dive for a Penny	Dog Paddle Relay	Duck Dive
Flag Relay	Frog Sub	Greased Watermelon
Innertube Relays	Innertube Water Polo	Jump or Dive
Keep Away	Leap Frog Relay	Marco Polo
Obstacle Relay	Over and Under	Partner Tag
Piggy Back	Races	Sharks and Minnows
Simon Says	Spoon/Egg Relay	Stunt Tag
Swimming Spelldown	Synchronized Swimming	Underwater Relay
Volleyball	Water Aerobics	Water Baseball
Water Basketball	Water Frisbee	Whirlpools

Arts/Crafts. Crafts enable youth to expand their creativity and imagination. Simple supplies can be used to make a variety of fun projects. The leader's role is to guide youth through the process of completing a project while encouraging creativity, innovation and individual expression. Ideally, youth will be excited about the end result as well as the process involved in creating their craft project. Following is an example of a craft project.

Fantasia Fish

Group Size	1 - 20	**Ages**	6 and up
Facility	Area with table	**Code**	N
Supplies	White cardboard or heavy paper, neon (glow in the dark) paint, paint brushes, scissors, dowels or sticks (2 feet long), paint shirts (optional), water, newspapers, tape or glue		
Directions	Put newspapers on work surface to protect it. Children design fish and other sea creatures and draw them on cardboard. Paint with neon paints. Cut out and tape or glue on the back. Turn out the lights and watch the deep sea come to life. This activity can also provide environmental education by supplying information and books on tropical fish and the coral reef.		
Safety	Be careful with scissors; they will need to be sharp ones to cut the cardboard.		
Theme	Have youth create a coral reef in the tropics.		

Types of Arts/Crafts Activities:

Beading	Birthday Cards	Picture Frames
Puff Paints	Body Tracing	Candles
Clay Play	Coat of Arms	Collages
Costume Making	Crayon Relief	Drawing
Egg Coloring	Family Tree	Finger Painting
Tie Dye	Friendship Pins	God's Eye
Ink Blowing	Leaf Prints	Ornaments
Mobiles	Murals	Painting
Paper Beads	Paper Mache	Party Decorations
Puppet Making	Cartooning	Rock Painting
Autograph Books	Bird Feeders	Book About Me
Adventure Authors	Pinata	Imitation Fossils
Paperweights	Masks	Medals
Paper Bag Puppets	Potato Block Prints	Sun Dials
Treasure Maps	Wool Weaving	Pennants

Drama. Drama activities allow youth to use their bodies and voices as a means of self-expression. Drama includes participatory activities such as games and storytelling and performance activities such as skits, recitation and magic tricks. Activities should provide 1) a range of roles to meet varied interests and talents 2) opportunities for creativity, innovation and individual expression and 3) gradual vehicles for youth to overcome inhibitions. Following is an example of a drama activity.

Pink Gorilla Story

Group Size	2-60	**Ages**	5 and up
Equipment	None	**Facility**	Any
Objective	To entertain a group	**Code**	B

Directions   Someone gets stranded near an old farm house and ends up sleeping in a barn until their car is repaired. The farmer warns the traveller that he is welcome to stay in the hayloft but under no circumstances should he touch the animal caged down the hallway. The traveller is very grateful and plans only to sleep but gets curious and decides to look at the animal, which is a pink gorilla. The traveller goes back to sleep, but is still curious and returns down the hallway to the gorilla again, this time *touching* it. In response the gorilla breaks out of his cage and chases the traveller who runs for his life across the United States. Eventually, the gorilla catches the exhausted traveller on the edge of the Grand Canyon thinking it's the end; as the gorilla approaches the traveller, the gorilla says "Tag, you're it!" and the storyteller tags the person next to them. *Variation:* For older children who are begging for a ghost story the barn can be a haunted house and the gorilla can be a ghost chasing with same result at the end.

Safety   If youth start to get scared, assure them that it will not be a scary ending.

Theme   Adapt the story so that it takes place on a journey through the rainforest.

Types of Drama Activities:

Charades	Creative drama
Festivals	Impersonations
Puppets	Pantomime
Shadow plays	Shows
Skits	Storytelling
Stunts	Demonstrations
Skit in a Bag	

Initiatives. An initiative activity is one that challenges the mental and/or physical abilities of the group. This type of activity requires the group to combine its efforts to complete the task. Initiatives will promote group interaction, cooperation, trust and belongingness. Initiatives include:

Knots

Group Size	6-15	**Ages**	8 and up
Equipment	None	**Facility**	Any
Objective	To form a circle without any twists	**Code**	C

Directions	Have the group stand shoulder to shoulder and form a circle, facing inward. Everyone reaches with their one hand and grabs the hand of someone else in the group. Then they reach out with their other hand and take another hand. The group then tries to form an untwisted circle without letting go of any hands. At the conclusion, this activity can be processed with questions which get the group to examine their roles in the group and how leadership was decided. Adaptation: try this sitting down!
Rules	Players must hold the hands of two different people and not the hands of the people standing next to them
Safety	None
Theme	Youth must learn to tie and untie knots for their journey through the tropics so they should start with this "human knot." Leaders who are good at knot tying could teach campers some simple knots after they untie themselves.

Types of Initiative Activities:

Data Processing	Touch My Can	Sherpa Walk
Hoop Pass	Blind Polygon	Trust Fall
Driving Miss Daisy	Human Knots	Magic Shoes
Partnering	Feets O Gee	Human Machine
Traffic Jam	Human Camera	Name Toss
Farkle Barkle		

Low Organized Games. Low organized games are characterized as those where most participants are involved in a low or moderate level of activity. They range from the subdued activities like riddles and brainteasers to circle games like "Duck, Duck, Goose." In most cases, an average- sized room will provide sufficient space.

Group Juggling

Group Size	6-15	**Ages**	6 and up
Equipment	4 - 6 soft balls	**Facility**	Any
Objective	To keep the balls in play	**Code**	C, N

Directions   Have the group stand in a circle facing inward. The group develops a sequence involving all players for how they are going to pass the ball. The first person tosses the ball to the designated person who passes it to the next designated person and so on. Once the group is comfortable with this, the first person adds a second ball and a third. The group tries to keep all the balls in play in the correct sequence.

Rules   When making the sequence, no player should pass the ball to a person standing next to them.

Safety   Everyone must throw the balls lightly to avoid injury.

Theme   Balls may represent threats to the rainforest. The group tries to see how many threats to the rainforest people can deal with before things begin to fall apart. Youth can then discuss how they can deal with the threats facing the rainforest today.

Types of Low Organized Games:

Animal, Vegetable, Mineral	Backward Walk	Bizz Buzz
Hip Charades	Checkers	Cookie Jar
Concentration	Electricity	Find the Penny
Hangman	Hot Potatoes	I Spy
I'm Going on a Hike	Let's Make a Deal	Wheel of Fortune
Mime	Mind Bogglers	Mind Reading
Minute Mysteries	Movies	Name the States
Poems	Progressive Story	Revolving Story
Rock, Paper, Scissors	Simon Says	Quiet Songs
Small Group Skits	Telephone	This is a What
Twenty Questions	Why and Because	Zoom
Wink	Time Bomb	Quick Draw

Music (Singing). Singing fosters spirit by involving all individuals in a unified effort. A good singing voice is not a requirement in order to have fun with music or lead a song successfully. Youth who are reticent to participate in the music program will often join in once they see their leaders enthusiastically involved and unafraid of looking "silly."

Supplementary music, such as instruments, adds an extra dimension to the music program. The music program is most dynamic when integrated into the general program and program theme:

Down by the Bay

Verses

Down by the bay where the watermelons grow
Back to my home I dare not go
For if I do my mother will say
<u>Have you ever seen a whale with a polka dotted tail?</u>
Down by the bay

<u>Have you ever seen a bear with pink underwear?</u>

<u>Have you ever seen potato grow from a tomato?</u>

<u>Have you ever seen a cow with a green eyebrow?</u>

<u>Have you ever seen a bee with a sore on his knee?</u>

<u>Have you ever seen a pig dancin' the Irish jig?</u>

Directions

Repeat the verse many times by changing the underlined line to different lines that participants make up. Make a contest out of it!

Types of Songs:

Alice the Camel	Alligator	America
Jaws	Barges	Bingo
Chocolate	Crazy Herman	Crocodile
Each Campfire	Eidelweiss	Eener Meener
Eskimo Sukada	Father Abraham	Five Hundred Miles
Found a Peanut	Four Leaf Clover	Frankenstein
Fried Ham	Ging Gang Gooli	Going on a Lion Hunt
Duke of York	Head and Shoulders	Hokey Pokey
If You're Happy	Little Pile of Tin	John Jacob
Bunny Foo Foo	Lollipop	Make New Friends
Michael Row	My Aunt Came Back	Peanut Butter
Princess Pat	Rocka-Chicka-Boom	Pruney
Sarasponda	Singing in the Rain	Sipping Cider
Spider Song	Swing Low	Ants Go Marching
We Are the World	Saints Go Marching	You Can't Get to Heaven

Nature. Nature activities help youth understand the world in which they live. A variety of activities can be incorporated into a nature program including games, experiments, hikes, stories and nature crafts. Nature games include:

Predator and Prey

Group Size	8-20	**Ages**	6 and up
Equipment	2 sealed containers with stones in them; 2 blindfolds	**Facility**	Any
Objective	For the predator to catch the prey	**Code**	N

Directions Discuss the natural phenomena of predators and prey. Have all but two people form a circle. The remaining two players are blindfolded and given 1 can which they use as a noise-maker. One is assigned to be the predator and the other the prey. Each is turned around in the circle so they do not know their position in relation to the other person. When the predator shakes the can, the prey must respond by doing the same. The players move around in the circle, the predator trying to follow the noise of the prey to tag it and the prey trying to escape by dodging out of the way. Once tagged, or after a certain amount of time passes, let two other people take on the roles in the circle. Let the players develop their own strategies.

Rules None

Safety The people forming the circle must keep the predator and prey safely inside.

Theme Youths will take on the role of animals. As each animal comes into the circle a predator or prey of that animal will also enter the circle and let nature take its course.

Types of Nature/Outdoor Activities:

Art Form Hunt	Chain Gang	Circle of Life
Directions Test	Making Soil	My Leaf
Nature Quiz	Peanut Patch	Pyramid of Life
Recipe for the World	Scavenger Hunt	Sense Hunting Games
Sensory Circle	Survival Circle	Tree Grokking
Tree-mendous Trees	Water Cycle	Web of Life

New Games. New Games are activities that are designed to allow children to have fun in a more non-competitive manner. The motto of the New Games approach is "Play Hard, Play Fair, Everybody Wins." New Games include:

Hagoo			
Group Size	8-20	**Ages**	6 and up
Equipment	None	**Facility**	Any
Objective	To make team members laugh	**Code**	N
Directions	Form two lines facing each other about three feet apart. One member from each team at opposite ends must walk the gauntlet passing in the middle. At the same time, members of each team attempt to make the other team member laugh or crack a smile (without physical contact). If either one of them smile, they must join the other's team line for the next passer-by.		
Rules	None		
Safety	The people forming the line must stay in line and not touch team members.		
Theme	Youth will take on the role of monkeys. As each monkey comes into the middle of the two lines, it will make monkey sounds and gestures, but cannot smile.		

Types of New Games:

Amoeba Race	Animal Tag	Aura
Band Aid Tag	Blob	Clumps
Dragon's Tail	Freeze Tag	Group Juggle
Group Stand Up	Group Sit	Human Pyramid
Islands	Knots	Leg Wrestling
Make Me Laugh	Partner Tag	People Pass
Prui	Run Octopus Run	Sheriffs/Bootleggers
Shoe Factory	Skin the Snake	Smaug's Jewels
Snake in the Grass	Spirals	Streets and Alleys
Trust Falls	TV Tag	Yurt Circle

Rainy Day. A rainy day package of activities, or "bag of tricks," should be available to each leader in case of inclement weather or some other unanticipated situation which interferes with the planned activities. This ensures that youth will not be idle and guarantees a stimulating program in spite of environmental limitations. The drudgery of showing videos, often over utilized as a "baby-sitter" can be avoided by being prepared to lead activities like the one listed:

Dutch Auction

Group Size	6-40	**Ages**	5 and up
Equipment	Paper and pencil	**Facility**	Any
Objective	To have the most items called by the leader	**Code**	None

Directions   Have the group divide into teams of 3-8 people, depending on the overall group size, and sit as a group. The leader prepares a list of items the participants might have on them or in their possession and calls them out one by one. Each team that can show they have the item, scores one point. The team with the most points in the end wins. This is a great activity on a rainy day! You may also present brainteasers (e.g. Wordless) that can earn points for each team.

Rules   Players may only take things that they can wear, but they may use pockets.

Safety   None

Theme   Inform youth that this game is going to test how well prepared they are as world travelers. Leaders should have wild uses for every item they call.

Types of Rainy Day Activities:

Rainy Day Smorgasbord	**Partner Tag**	**Drawing in the Dark**
Rhythm	**Thumb Buddy**	**Star Wars**
A What?	**Orchestra**	**Profile Painting**
Killer		

Special Events. A special event may conclude a themed week or month on a high note and allow youth and staff closure on their experience. Special events should be theme related which should allow staff to build up to this event during the month or week's activities. Special events are usually longer program periods and should involve the entire community. Following is an example of a special event.

Carnival

Group Size	20 - 100 **Ages** 6 and up
Equipment	Picnic tables, old boxes, paper, crayons, magic markers, scissors, tape, aluminum foil, etc.
Facility	Large open area
Procedure	Have each small group plan and organize one booth at the earth carnival. Booths may include: face painting, tree planting, environmental trivia, making recycled paper, rainforest mural, creating a letter (with drawings) that campers could sign and send to a mayor, senator, etc., recycling garbage at camp, fishing for facts, or making animal puppets. Encourage groups to be creative with their booths and try to use recyclable material in creating each booth.
Safety	Make sure leaders are placed strategically to ensure adequate supervision during the event.

Types of Special Events:

Holidays	Winter Carnival
Spring Spectacular	Summer Carnival
Battle of the bands	Art show
Hobby show	Craft show
Film festival	Junior Olympics
Table tennis tournament	Baseball card show
Fishing derby	Bicycle Derby
Bubble gum blowing contest	Cultural celebrations
Watermelon seed spitting contest	Pie eating contest
Egg throwing contest	Treasure hunt
Sports skills contests	Scavenger hunt
Fifties day	Backwards day
Star Trek day	Pet show/Unusual pet show

Sports. Athletics is an important component of the youth program. This is even more critical in today's world when children are maintaining increasingly sedentary lifestyles. Athletics can increase motor skills, enhance self-esteem and teach sportsmanship, teamwork and *healthy* competition. Following is an example of a sporting event.

Soccer Baseball

Equipment 1 rubber ball; 4 bases (optional)   **Facility**: Gym/Outside
Objective To score the most runs   **Code**   None

Directions   Divide into 2 teams. One team plays "in the field" while the other bats. The pitcher throws or bounces the ball to the batter who kicks it into the field. The outfield team must control the ball without using their hands and kick it to three other players and kick a goal. If the goal is made before the runner crosses home plate, the runner is out. One goalie from the batting team is allowed to try to stop the goal. If the runner makes it back to home plate before the basket is made, a run is scored. Teams switch places after three outs or a pre-determined number of runs is reached. Small groups: Children bat and staff field.

Rules: Each player must bat on their turn; if a player throws the bat, then the player is out.
If the attempted goal is missed, any player in the field may rebound and try again.
Foul balls are not playable; keeping track of strikes is optional.

Safety   With younger players, the activity leader may want to do all the pitching and goal keeping.

Theme   Youth get to try a new game that is a cross between baseball and soccer.

Types of Sports:

Individual Sports	Dual sports	Team Sports	
Golf	Tennis	Baseball	Softball
Bowling	Badminton	Basketball	Football
Swimming	Handball	Volleyball	Crab Soccer
Tumbling	Racquetball	Soccer	Keep Away
Skating	Kickball	HackySack	Floor Hockey
Skiing	Dodgeball	Ultimate Frizbee	
Hiking			
Track and Field			

Trips. Trips are an important feature of some youth programs. Field trips provide a change of scenery, an opportunity to learn new things, and facilities and specialized personnel not usually available. Possible field trip options include: zoos, amusement parks, museums, parks, roller-skating rinks, bowling, lakes, sporting events, and industry tours.

ACTIVITIES THAT BUILD SELF-ESTEEM
AND SELF-CONFIDENCE

Following are activities that can be used by the youth leader to help youth build self-esteem and to support diverse programs. Youth that feel a sense of belonging to the group and a sense of self-esteem are less likely to act out in negative ways, and more likely to develop in a positive manner. In addition, there is an indication that feelings of prejudice toward others are most likely to occur in persons who do not feel good about themselves. Following are suggestions of self-esteem-building activities as adapted from Mueller and Webber (1990).

Circle Game. All youth sit in a circle with one person in the middle. All youth in the circle write a positive comment on a piece of paper (that has been cut into circles, squares, triangles, or other creative shapes) about the youth. The youth in the middle collects all the pieces of paper and reads them aloud, then uses them to make collage or a mobile to hang in their room at home. Each youth gets a turn in the middle.

Compliments. Have the group share with each other: "I'd like to have [this attribute] of yours."

Fingerprints. Provide paper or cardboard and an ink pad, make fingerprints. Allow youth to study and compare their fingerprints using magnifying glasses. See if students can pick their own prints out of the batch of them. Discuss everyone's uniqueness. This activity is a good lead in to a discussion of individual qualities and strengths. Fingerprints may be used in a group poster or self-collage.

Graffiti. Have each child make a poster with his/her name on it, and some symbols about him/herself. Invite other youth to write positive comments on the posters whenever they notice something special about that individual. Or, pass the poster around the group in a circle and have each person write a positive comment on each other person's poster.

Autobiographies. Sharing the significant moments of one's life with others can be very affirming for the individual, while it promotes deeper communication and trust. Make sure that children listen and pay attention to one another.

Pairing Activities. Have youth ask each other — Who are you? What is good about you? What do you hope for?

Name Game. Youth sit in a circle. The leader begins by saying I'm Sally. The next person says, I'm Joe and that's Sally (pointing). The next person says, I'm Andre, that's Joe, and that's Sally. Continue until the last person can name everyone in the group. In the second round repeat the process, but have each individual add a positive adjective to their name beginning with the same letter as their name — Sweet Sally, Awesome Andre. Then continue as before, I'm Awesome Andre, that's Sweet Sally, and so on.

Movie Time. Give youth time to recall significant moments in their lives. Ask them to imagine that a Hollywood producer is making a movie of their life. Ask them to decide what the movie title would be — a title that would sum up their lives to this point. After about 30 seconds to think, give them 2 minutes to tell their life story (the plot of the movie) beginning with the title. Other variations of this would be to have youth write out or draw out the story first and then share it. Or, to do a video of themselves and capture the unique story of each person talking and interacting on videotape.

TOTAL QUALITY
PROGRAM PLANNING CHECKLIST

During the *program development* phase of program planning, the youth leader is responsible for coordinating a number of details. Following are some of the tasks that the leader must identify and organize during this phase of program planning. These will be found later in a planning form.

✓　　**Select program area and specific program/activity.** After needs assessment and review of youth development factors and youth input, the leader selects the programs and activities that will be offered.

✓   **Select type of program format.** The program format is defined (class, drop-in, competitive, club, outreach, interest group, special event).

✓   **Set the program date/location.** The leader must make a final decision on date(s) and location.

✓   **Justification of need.** The leader must justify the provision of the service. In other words, the leader must indicate why he/she believes the service is needed and warranted.

✓   **Program objectives/action steps.** During the program development stage of the planning process, the leader specifies the actions steps that will be necessary to accomplish the program objectives that were developed in Step three of the planning model. Program objectives and the action steps to carry them out enable the youth leader to connect youth needs with the organization's resources. They provide a way to connect means and ends; that is, "What resources will be used in order to produce what result?" Program objectives must be specific, measurable and have a dimension of time. They concern the benefits to be realized by participants in the program.

✓   **Methods of publicity.** The leader will also need to determine which methods of publicity will be used to promote the program. Newspaper ads, press releases, brochures, flyers, posters, bulletin boards, radio/TV, and other means for publicity are available. Publicity will be discussed in depth later in this section.

✓   **Participant Information.** The number of participants, their ages and sex, must also be determined during the program development stage of planning. These factors may influence the way in which the program is organized and implemented.

✓   **Facility Requirements.** The physical set up of the facility will need to be determined, as well as requirements for ordering set up services, e.g. sound system, set -up for tables and chairs, other.

✓ **Participant Safety Issues.** Certain participant safety issues must be considered, including experience of participants, collection of permission slips, risk management of on-site hazards, emergency phone numbers and other relevant factors.

✓ **Leadership.** The individuals who will lead the program must be identified by name, including staff, volunteers, others.

✓ **Transportation.** Transportation needs should be considered and organized, and the distance to the location also considered.

✓ **Equipment and Supplies.** The leader will need to make a list of equipment and supplies required for the program, and obtain them.

✓ **Program Costs.** Program costs for leadership, facilities, equipment, transportation, supplies, promotion and other related costs need to be determined, in advance, and approved by a supervisor.

✓ **Clearance coordination.** A number of clearances may need to be obtained, Including clearance/approval from a supervisor, clearance for use of a facility, parent permission, and other specialized clearances.

✓ **Special supplies.** Finally, the leader may need to round up a number of special supplies — prizes, decorations, invitations, refreshments.

✓ **Program fees.** Some programs require that a fee be charged to offset program costs. The youth leader must determine whether or not a program fee will be charged and, if so, the justification for it.

Total Quality Program Planning Form. A Total Quality Program Planning Form, containing the tasks discussed in this section follows . . .

TOTAL QUALITY PROGRAM
PLANNING FORM

EMPLOYEE: **PROGRAM DATE:**

ACTIVITY: _____ (Descriptive Title)

LOCATION: _____ (Facility Name/Address)

TYPE OF PROGRAM: **JUSTIFICATION OF NEED:**

____ Continuous   ____ Carryover from previous activity

____ Special   ____ Expansion of previous activity

____ Annual   ____ Youth/Parent Survey

____ Other   ____ Established Standards

                             ____ Suggestion Program

                             ____Available Expert Leadership

                             ____ Speculation

                             ____ Other - Specify

PROGRAM OBJECTIVES: (Continue on Separate Page if Needed)

1. _____

_____

2. _____

_____

3. _____

_____

ACTION STEPS:

1. _____

_____

2. _____

   _____

3. _____

   _____

4. _____

   _____

5. _____

(Be specific — detail exactly what has to be done to plan and implement the program, step-by-step, including a detailed outline of what activities are to occur, when and who would be in charge. Use separate page if needed.)

METHODS OF PUBLICITY

____ Newspaper Ad

____ Press Release

____ Photographs

____ Brochures

____ Special Emblem

____ Exhibition

____ Demonstrations

____ Buttons/Decals/Banner

____ Word of Mouth

____ Flyers

Posters

____ Radio/Television

____ Film/Slides

PARTICIPANTS/ESTIMATED NUMBER:

____ Male

____ Female

____ Adults - Specify Ages ____

____ Youths - Specify Ages ____

____ Special Characteristics

____ **FACILITY REQUIREMENTS:**

_____

_____

(Physical Set-up, Arrangements)

PARTICIPANT SAFETY:

_____ Abilities, qualifications, experiences of participants.

_____Special Policies

_____ Permission slips for participants

_____ Identifiable hazards

_____Emergency services/ phone numbers

_____ Staff preparation/ training

LEADERSHIP:

____ Staff members (names)　　_____

____ Volunteers (names)　　_____

____ Paid Officials (names)　　_____

____ Others - Specify　　_____

TRANSPORTATION REQUIRED:

EQUIPMENT/SUPPLIES/ OTHER ITEMS NEEDED:

_____　　_____

_____　　_____

_____　　_____

_____　　_____

(Distance to Location)　　_____

**CLEARANCE/
COORDINATION**

PROGRAM COSTS:

_____ Supervisor

$ _____ Leadership

_____ Facility

$ _____ Facility

_____ Parent Permission

$ _____ Equipment

_____ Scheduling

$ _____ Transportation

_____ Other-Specify

$ _____ Supplies

$ _____ Promotion

$ _____ Other-Specify

TOTAL COST: $

**SPECIAL SUPPLIES AND
ARRANGEMENTS:**

**PROGRAM FEES AND
JUSTIFICATION:**

_____ Prizes

_____

_____

_____ Invitations

_____

_____ Decorations

_____

_____ Refreshments

_____ Room Set-Up

PROGRAM PROMOTION

Program promotion is a vital part of the work of a youth leader engaged in program development. It is geared not only toward informing participants about programs, activities and events, but it is involved with representing the organization to the public and higher officials in such a way that financial support is maintained or enhanced.

Marketing your youth programs and services is a key element to their success. Use of the media, brochures, flyers and other tools, will help you promote your program offerings and attract youth to participate in them.

Following are methods you can use to get your message out.

✓   **Publicity/Advertising**. Depending on the type, size and scope of your program, your program promotion may range from passing out and posting flyers and posters, to generating newsletter coverage, newspaper articles, radio and television spots and other means.

✓   **Flyers/Brochures/Bulletin Boards.** Flyers and brochures can be an effective means for sending your message to youth and their parents. Bulletin boards can also present information in an effective manner. Suggestions for preparing promotional materials, such as flyers are included later in this section.

How and where should you distribute flyers? Schools, grocery stores, the youth center, parents' clubs, home mailings and other means are effective ways to distribute flyers and brochures.

✓   **Newspapers**. Newspapers are an excellent way to market programs and to let youth and their parents know about available programs. Newspapers often have a section in which they provide an update on activities in the community. In addition, you can submit information and pictures to them for special features about your programs and services.

Your chances of obtaining newspaper coverage are greater if you develop a good working relationship with one or two reporters, and if you help them by providing an initial draft news release and pictures that they can use as a basis for an article.

✓   **Newsletters.** Any newsletters in the community can be used to get your message across regarding youth programs and services.

✓   **Welcome Packets.** Chamber of Commerce, as well as large area business welcome packets should include current, updated information about your youth programs and services, so that youth who are new to the community can learn about your organization's offerings. The information should be presented in a dynamic, professional, effective manner so as to interest youth and their parents.

✓   **Personal Contact.** You can spread the word about your programs and services through personal contact. Talking with youth and their parents, speaking to various clubs and organizations can inform people about what is available from your organization.

✓   **Posters.** Posters displayed strategically at areas where youth and their parents are likely to see them, will get out the word about your programs and services. Schools, grocery stores, youth centers, bus stops, bookstores, restaurants, and other locations that are high traffic are good sites for putting up posters.

✓   **Radio/TV.** Both radio and television organizations are interested in providing public service announcements, in order to inform their listeners. They want information about your programs and services. However, it is up to you to keep them informed. They will not usually come looking for you.

The organizations that receive extensive publicity about their programs and services usually generate that publicity themselves. They develop a relationship with individuals in the media, and they submit information to them. You will be more likely to gain coverage of your events and services if you write the news release yourself, so that it is easy for the media to process it and use it.

Preparing Promotional Materials

Although youth service staff should coordinate with their organization's marketing department to market and advertise programs, with today's computers youth leaders can also engage in desktop publishing to prepare preliminary advertisements, flyers, and other materials.

- Headlines should be *action-oriented and brief*. If possible, they should attempt to involve the reader. *Use of the word "you" involves the reader* to a greater degree. In addition, the language should relate to the audience. For example, if the flyer is directed to a young person; think about how kids that age really talk and what they think is fun.

  Make sure that the programs you are planning and your flyers and brochures *relate to what young people really want to do*. Is your language developmentally appropriate or age-appropriate? Interest appropriate?

- The publication should be *specific in its purpose*. Before you develop your materials ask yourself "Why am I developing this?" "What is the purpose?" "Who is it directed to?" If you are sending a flyer about a specific program, then stick to that. Don't add in other messages that are not related; this confuses the reader.

- When sending out flyers about programs, use the standard *"Who, What, Why, Where and When,"* to inform your reader about the basic information he/she needs to know.

- Use key phrases that are *meaningful to young people.* Youth want to be involved in things that are fun and exciting, that are worthwhile, that will allow them to socialize with others, that offer opportunities for teamwork, that offer opportunities for being a part of something larger than they are, that offer opportunities for recognition and achievement, that offer opportunities for growth and learning, and that offer opportunities to give to others.

- Be *careful in your use of clip art.* Make sure that it represents your ideas effectively; poor clip art confuses and detracts from your message.

- Use *simple, clear type.* Old English, script and other ornate type may detract from the professionalism of your message. Use these types of techniques only if they relate to the theme of your flyer.

- Your message should be *easy to read and brief.* People will spend a short period of time, less than a minute scanning your flyer or poster. Ask yourself what information you would include if your message was going to be viewed for 10 seconds. Also, what order should you use to display your information; e.g. put the most important information first, or highlight it so it stands out.

- The *size of type* will vary with the type of flyer or brochure. The headlines should be 18-24 point and the descriptive text should be a minimum of 12-14 point.

- Keep your flyers, posters and brochures *uncluttered.* If your audience has to search for your message they won't read it. Keep it simple and clean. Don't use too much clip art or text.

- Establish a *resource file folder* of your flyers, posters, brochures, and news releases and articles for future reference.

- The paper that you use should represent the idea that you are trying to convey. Bright colors indicate excitement and fun. Beiges and brown make a professional, dignified statement. Use a good quality of paper. Cheap, poorly printed materials will reflect on the quality of your organization and its programs.

Creating Advertising Appeal for Youth

Young people do not have preconceived notions. Advertising for youth can be completely creative and innovative. Following are suggestions for creating appeal for youth in your printed materials, as adapted from Jan Hoppe (1990).

Element	Comments
Color	Color is one of the strongest interest grabbers for youth. Through about age four, young people prefer bright primary colors (blue, red, green, yellow). After that they develop favorites, but solid bright colors are always safe. A color many kids dislike is "Mr. Yuk" green. That is why it was chosen to "repulse" kids.
Illustration or photography	Interesting visuals are worth a "thousand words." Cartoons are a special favorite. Mix photography with line art, cartoons, and realistic drawings. Straight photography or realistic art can look too businesslike.
Humor	You will be surprised how effective humor can be in teaching! Cartoons and silly jokes will draw more attention than the best printed copy.

| Comfortable | Keep sentences crisp, clean, relatively short. Limit   reading level to three and four syllable words. Eliminate unnecessary words. Sound natural in your writing. Check it by reading your material out loud; do youth talk like that? |

| Take an Unusual View | Capitalize on curiosity. Be creative! Need a picture of a tree?   Take it   from   the ground looking up.   Challenge creative thinking with questions that ask "What if...?" |

| Offer Active Learning | Do you like reading sentences about things, or would you rather do learning activities? Replace lengthy text with: crossword puzzles, word search games, hidden   pictures, riddles, mazes, pencil puzzles and more. |

Creating Advertising Appeal for Youth

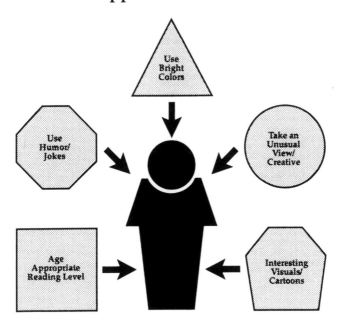

Personal Notes:
Program Development

What are three different program formats that you may use in programming? What format would you choose for the program area of basketball?

_____

_____

There are five activity clusters from which the youth leader may select daily programs and activities in order to offer variety in programming and to promote the attainment of youth development competencies. What are these, and how does the leader use them?

a)   d)

b)   e)

c)

What are some of the things that the leader can do to help youth feel valued?

_____

_____

Use the format below to create an activity card that can be used as part of your "bag of tricks" as you work with youth.

Title:

Group size: _____   Age: _____

Equipment: _____   Facility:_____

Objective: _____   Code: _____

Directions: _____

_____

Rules: _____

_____

Safety: _____

_____

Theme: _____

_____

_____

References

Edginton, C.R., C.J. Hansen and S.R. Edginton (1992). *Leisure Programming: Concepts, Trends, and Professional Practice.* Dubuque, IA: Brown and Benchmark.

DeGraaf, D. G. and K. H. DeGraaf. (1994). *U.S. Army Youth Services Training Guide: Planning and Supervising Camp Programs.* Cedar Falls, IA: University of Northern Iowa.

Hoppe, J. (1990). Creating Ad Appeal For Youth. In J. Cantress (1991). *Curriculum Development for Issues Programming.* Washington,D.C.: U.S.Department of Agriculture.

Mueller, C. and Webber, M. (1990). *Celebrating Diversity: A Manual for Bringing Multicultural Education to Youth Work.* St. Louis, MO: Anti-Defamation League.

CHAPTER 14

Program Implementation

Program implementation is the period of time during which the program or activity that the youth leader has planned actually takes place. At this time, the leader is with youth and the program or service is unfolding. The *program implementation* step of the program planning model involves getting youth involved in programs and activities, and *keeping them involved.*

This chapter of the book offers information regarding this fifth step in the program planning process — program implementation. The *program implementation* step in the planning process involves the leader's interaction with youth and other customers, leadership considerations, including behavior management, as well as safety issues and risk management.

As a result of reading this chapter, you will be able to:

▶ Gain an understanding of the topic of leadership, including leadership style and characteristics of effective leaders.

▶ Learn methods for leading activities, behavior management, conflict resolution, and promoting youth leadership.

▶ Increase the safety of youth through risk management.

On the following page is the *program implementation* step as it appears in the program planning diagram.

Major sections of this chapter were contributed by Dr. Donald DeGraaf, Kathy DeGraaf, Dr. Debra Jordan, and Dr. Sue Koch. Dr. Don DeGraaf and Kathy DeGraaf contributed the material on the topics of general leadership guidelines, child abuse, and how to prevent behavior problems and handle youth with special needs. Dr. Debra Jordan provided the material on the topic of risk management, and Dr. Sue Koch contributed the material on conflict resolution.

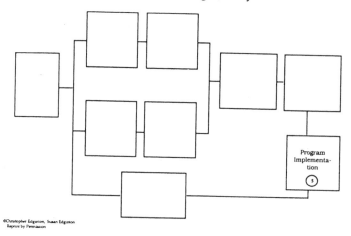

The youth leader will need many skills at this point in the program process. Knowledge regarding behavior management, how to lead songs and games, how to handle complaints, and other related information is essential. Some of the activities that take place during this step of the program planning process are:

❑   General Leadership

❑   Helping Youth Feel Valued

❑   Promoting Youth Leadership/Involvement

❑   Implementing a Plan of Customer Service

❑   Handling Complaints

❑   Behavior Management

❑   Risk Management

The youth leader will act in many roles at this point in the program process. Knowledge of how to provide excellence in customer service, step-by-step instructions regarding how to lead songs and games, how to handle complaints, and other related information is essential.

GENERAL LEADERSHIP GUIDELINES

The key person in providing a positive experience for youth is the leader. This section of the book will focus on developing and fine tuning the direct face-to-face leadership skills needed most by youth leaders.

Three Types of Leadership Style

There has been much information written about leadership and leadership style. However, three basic types of leadership have been identified and include:

❏ **Authoritarian**. The leader makes all the decisions. The leader usually dictates the particular task for each group member.

❏ **Democratic**. The leader attempts to build group consensus on all decisions made by the group. All policies are a matter of group discussion and decision, encouraged and assisted by the leader.

❏ **Laissez-Faire**. The leader allows the group total freedom to make decisions. Complete nonparticipation by the leader in the group process.

Leaders who are task-oriented are said to be concerned with getting specific objectives accomplished. Leaders who are process-oriented are said to be more concerned with the dynamics that go on within the group rather than accomplishing specific objectives. Within the three basic styles of leadership discussed above, authoritarian leaders tend to be more task-oriented while democratic leaders tend to be more process-oriented.

Which Leadership Style is the "Correct" One?

This question has long been studied in youth-related settings. In the early 1930s, a landmark study was conducted that examined which of the three leadership styles listed above was most effective when working with children (Lewin, Lippit and White, 1939). Through a series of studies, the researchers compared the effects of the three types of leadership on groups of boys. Most of the boys were apathetic to the autocratic leadership and reported liking the democratic leadership best. Laissez-faire leaders were reported as being all right.

One result of this early study is that many leisure service texts suggest that a democratic leadership style is most desirable and effective in all situations. However, more recent studies on leadership have suggested there is no one ideal leadership style. *Leadership is dependent on the situation (environment), the people involved (their skill level, maturity level, etc.) and group dynamics* (Edginton and Ford, 1985). This means that leaders must be flexible and have the ability to step back from situations to analyze and try new things.

Thus in a case where youth safety is an issue, an authoritarian approach to leadership may be warranted. Whereas a more democratic approach may be used when helping a small group decide what they want to do as a group for a talent show at the end of the week. Good leaders must learn to match their leadership style to their situation, their personality, and the task at hand.

WHAT MAKES AN EXCEPTIONAL YOUTH LEADER?

The answer to the question "What makes an exceptional youth leader?" depends on who is answering the question. Youth, parents, and supervisors may vary considerably in what they perceive as being the most important qualities of a youth leader. For example, while everyone might agree that being a "fun" person is important, this may rank far higher on the youths' list than the adults. Likewise, for parents and administrators, being safety conscious may be the most important quality for an exceptional youth leader, whereas for youth this may be a less important trait.

Research in the youth services field has demonstrated that one quality upon which both adults and youth agree as being an important trait for youth leaders is being accepting of children. Youth are more likely to improve their self-concept, have a "fun" experience and learn positive behaviors when they perceive their leaders are accepting of them. According to Chenary (1985) a youth sees a counselor as accepting when the counselor:

❑ Likes to talk with me and be with me much of the time;

❑ Smiles at me a lot;

❑ Tries to treat me as an equal;

❑ Isn't interested in changing me, but likes me as I am;

❑ Seems to see my good points more than my faults;

❑ Doesn't mind if I "kid" him/her about things;

❑ Is very interested in what I am learning in activities; and

❑ Tries to understand how I see things.

Leadership Considerations — The eight great "ates"

It is important that youth leaders identify the qualities they see as important. Following are tips for the youth leader as reported by Michael Brandwein (1989), called the eight great "ates" because they all end in "ate."

- **Motivates**. Staff must be prepared to do a good job, requiring a lot of hard work, and their attitude must reflect this. One inexperienced staff member with the right attitude is worth far more than the most skilled leader with the wrong attitude.

  Youth leaders must motivate youth by actively participating. Leaders must excite youth to get involved and set the standard. If the youth leader is excited, youth will be excited. Maintain a good attitude. Positive attitudes are important and contagious. Be enthusiastic and energetic and it will rub off on participants.

- **Communicates.** To be a good communicator leaders must learn to listen. In many areas of life children are expected to be quiet (i.e. the old adage: "children should be seen and not heard"). However, youth programs should be different. Leaders should try to create an environment where children feel free to express themselves. Leaders need to treat children as people worthy of their time and attention.

  To facilitate this awareness leaders can ask themselves: What was the longest conversation I had with a youth today? What was it about? Have a question for the day built into the program. Sample questions include: What do you dream about? What would you do if you ran this youth center? Have kids come up with their own questions to ask each other or to ask leaders.

- **Accommodates.** Staff must be able to get along with others. It is important to develop a "we" feeling in youth programs (i.e. "we" can do wonders; "we" can solve any problem or challenge). Leaders who are willing to accommodate others, demonstrate a willingness and ability to compromise. They support the ideas of other team members and remain flexible in times of stress or conflict. Cooperative staff are more likely to produce cooperative youths.

- **Anticipates.** Leaders can learn to anticipate both the needs of youth as well as problems which may arise. Anticipating the needs of youth allows leaders to plan for these needs. Likewise leaders can learn to anticipate problems and deal with them in a pro-active manner rather than in a reactive manner. Such leaders are usually able to contain problems rather than see them escalate. Anticipate dangers; think like a child.

- **Facilitates.** Leaders must help youth take ownership of their youth center experience. Leaders who facilitate experiences for children allow them to make their own decisions about such things as skits, youth shows, etc. It means making sure the needs of the youth are met.

- **Creates.** Leaders must create a caring environment for children to grow as individuals. Youth Centers can be microcosms of the real world where youth can learn about democracy, a place where they can see their role in a larger community.

- **Educates.** Leaders are first and foremost role models for youth. With this in mind, leaders must remember that everything they do involves education; they can teach by being positive role models, thereby leading by example. Play is a powerful tool in the hands of leaders. Through play, youth can learn valuable lessons if leaders recognize these opportunities and use them wisely.

- **Celebrates.** Demonstrate genuine excitement. Have fun! If leaders do not enjoy their job it will be a long year, but if they do enjoy their job it can be one of the best years of their life. Freely express joy in life and the current moment. Openly participate in all activities; demonstrate genuine excitement and celebrate life!

Other possible "ate" words include: participates, validates, initiates, dedicates, cooperates, recreates, concentrates, differentiates, liberates, dictates, demonstrates.

METHODS FOR TEACHING AND LEADING ACTIVITIES

The leadership traits listed above present broad concerns of which all youth center leaders should be aware. The list below is more of a "nuts and bolts" approach which presents a systematic method of teaching and leading activities within the youth center setting. This list discussed by DeGraaf and DeGraaf (1994)was designed to help leaders become aware of the way they relate to youth, and to give them specific things to practice.

✓ **Use a variety of ways to obtain the attention of the group:** Some innovative ways to capture youths' attention include:

- **Theme phrase.** Create a theme-related phrase each week as a cue to quiet down. Youth should know to repeat this phrase whenever leaders yell the first part of it (i.e. during the Underwater Adventure theme week leaders may want to use the phrase "Splish Splash" whereby leaders yell *"Splish"* and the youths yell back *"Splash"*);

- **Catchy sayings.** Utilize other catchy sayings as a cue for the group to quiet down (i.e. have leaders yell "Hip Hip Hip" and the youths yell back "popotamus");

- **Actions.** Have youths do a specific action as a cue for the group to quiet down (i.e. clap *three* times if you can hear me, clap *twice* if you can hear me). Say the instruction very softly so only a few youths do the action initially, with their response soon catching the attention of the whole group;

- **Word of the Day.** Develop a *Word of the Day* or week so that when youths hear it, they can yell and scream for five seconds and then get quiet;

- **Hand over Head.** Develop a standard action like the hand over the head, whereby when the hand goes up, youth are quiet;

- **Routines.** Develop a routine where youths know what is expected of them at certain times (i.e. one leader started every day off with a rousing *Goooooooood Moooooorning*. Once this was said the youths knew to answer back *Goooooood Moooorning, Ron*, thereby starting the day).

✓ **Know your group**. Memorize names as quickly as possible. Adjust your activities to the abilities and interests of the group.

✓ **Position yourself for giving directions.** Make sure everyone can hear you. Stay in front of the group; never place yourself in the middle of a group. Do not allow participants to be behind you during any explanations. Try not to have youths looking into the sun when giving directions. Make appropriate eye contact to assess if youths are understanding what you are talking about.

✓ **Understand and know the rules of the game.** Try to keep rules to a minimum. Avoid repetition in the explanation.

✓ **Have equipment ready.** Set up all equipment for your activities before you begin.

✓ **Demonstrate the game whenever possible.** Ask for questions to make sure everyone understands the instructions before beginning the activity. Avoid yes/no questions.

✓ **Pick fair teams.** Children have a keen sense of fairness and want to have opportunities to win. Leaders need to develop a number of unique ways to break participants into smaller groups that make the team-choosing process fun in and of itself. Some examples of unique ways to divide a large group into smaller teams include:

- **Close your eyes**. Have group on a straight line and have one half of the group take two steps forward and one half of the group take two steps backwards.

- **Play the game** *Mingle*. Begin by shouting out "mingle" which cues everyone to mingle around greeting and visiting with each other while keeping an ear tuned to the leader's next direction. Have everyone get into smaller units, such as groups of 3, by shouting out the corresponding number. Once everyone is in a group of 3 have the entire group mingle again and then get into groups of 5. Have the group mingle again and then get into the size groups you need for your activity. One consideration when using this method is knowing the total number of youths involved, so that groups are even without leaving anyone without a group.

- **Pick a partner.** (Sometimes you can give more specific directions such as: Pick a partner with a similar shoe size as you. Pick a partner your height, and so on). One partner is on one team the other partner on the other team.

- **Those who like.** Have the group stand in a straight line with their eyes closed and have them think about a giant M&M. Those who see a plain M&M should step backward while those who see a peanut M&M should step forward. This can be done with other choices as well.

- **Have youth look at their fingernails.** All those whose palm is facing up go to one side; all those whose palm is facing down go to the other side.

- **Birthday months.** January to June birthdays are on one side. July to December birthdays are on the other side   This can be altered by having everyone born in April, July, September, June, etc., on one side (keep adding months until you have enough people on one side).

- **Clasp your hands.** Everyone whose right thumb is on top go to one side, those whose left thumb is on top go to the other side.

These methods may leave you with unequal sides, however you as a leader can continue to manipulate the teams until they are equal.

✓ **Challenge youth**. Emphasize competition against self (i.e. improving their skills and reaching their potential) when competition is necessary. Challenge youths to play fair and by the rules.

✓ **Keep games fresh and new**. Use objects that are unfamiliar to players. When leaders use footballs, basketballs, and softballs in the conventional way children have preconceived notions of the game itself (i.e. if a basketball is brought out and a youth is short they immediately think they can't play). If you use equipment in unique ways, participants have no preconceived notions about how the game is to be played. Another way to keep games fresh and new is to tie activities into different themes and playing them a little differently.

✓ **Keep participants playing.** Don't include rules that permanently eliminate players. Find creative ways to get youths back into elimination type games.

✓ **Be involved and actively supervise the activity**. Decide on the role of the leader before the activity starts. Different roles include:

- **Observer**. Should you observe to get a better feel for the group? For safety reasons?

- **Active Player**. Should you involve yourself in the game? Can you maintain control of the situation if you actively play?
- **Passive Player.** Should you be involved by giving positive feedback and support to players?

- **Safety monitor**. Should you simply monitor safety concerns for the group?

The leader's role may change with the situation, the game, and the group. Be alert to clues which will direct your role.

✓ **Monitor the flow of the game**. Keep activities moving. Be willing to make adaptations to facilitate the success of the activity. Don't be afraid to change the rules to fit your situation.

✓ **Monitor safety considerations.** Leaders should be concerned with the emotional, social, and physical safety of each member of the group. Constantly monitor the situation and the environment to assure a safe experience for youths.

✓ **Bring closure to the activity.** Always quit a game at its height of popularity. This ensures that youths will not become bored by the activity and will want to come back and play the game at a later time.

✓ **Consider the transitions into the next activity**. Before one game ends think through how the next game will begin or how youths will get to the next activity area.

HOW TO PREVENT BEHAVIOR PROBLEMS

The issue of discipline of youth is extremely complicated and often controversial for a variety of reasons. In order to develop a meaningful behavior management strategy, several things must happen which include making a commitment to prevention. *A firm commitment to prevention of severe behavior problems is the best behavior management plan of all.* Examples of preventive techniques according to DeGraaf and DeGraaf (1994) include:

❑   **A reward system** whereby youth earn something desirable for positive behavior.

❑   **Clear expectations** regarding behavior and noncompliance to rules.

❑   **A well-planned, innovative program** which keeps youths occupied in productive tasks.

❑   **Adequate supervision** of youths by leaders and leaders by administration.

❑   **Signals** that let everyone know when it's time to get serious and pay attention; including youth input into decision making.

Other actions that help the youth leader establish and carry out a well-ordered, effective behavior management strategy include the following.

❑ **Create Policies.** *Establish and communicate the program's policies regarding youth behavior and staff intervention.* These should be shared with all parties involved, including seasonal staff, youth and parents prior to the beginning of programs.

This should involve both group discussion as well as written materials which address both general philosophy and specific policies (e.g. no corporal punishment is allowed at any time; any suspicion of child abuse occurring at home is *immediately* reported to the youth center director).

❑ **Acknowledge Differences.** *Exchange of ideas among youth center staff regarding personal discipline styles through* the use of group discussion is important, especially for leaders who share leadership/supervision responsibilities. Does the leader tend to deal with the behavior itself, an underlying problem which seems to be causing the undesired behavior, or both?

❑ **Balance the Needs of all Youth.** Determine *at what point the needs of the youth center staff or the group outweigh the needs of an individual youth.* At times leaders react prematurely with requests to "get rid of a youth" who is causing problems in the group. While different intervention strategies should be discussed and tried, equally important is an evaluation of how the problematic youth is affecting the entire group.

A request to "suspend" a youth who is inconvenient and/or requires more energy than most is not legitimate; however, if a youth's problematic behavior is impacting on the experience of the other youths to a point that they are unable to have a positive experience, then removing the youth from the group must be seriously considered.

❑ **Develop Natural Consequences.** Natural and logical consequences of misbehavior should be utilized whenever possible. *Natural consequences are those accrued as a direct result of an individual's behavior.* For example, if youth take an inordinate amount of time lining up for transitions from one activity to another, they will have less activity time.

❑ **Establish a Progression of Interventions.** *Less adverse consequences should precede those most severe.* If a youth is disrupting the group by talking while the leader is giving instructions, the first approach should be the least intrusive and then build to the more serious interventions if the misbehavior does not cease.

For example, try simply making eye contact with the youth to let them know that you are aware of their behavior and would like it to stop. If that doesn't work, a progression such as moving physically closer to the youth, addressing the youth by name, giving a verbal warning, and then a "time-out" could be tried in this order. Eye contact is generally ineffective and no longer an option if a "time-out" is given initially so leaders are severely limiting their options to start at the more serious end of the spectrum.

❑ **Create Support Networks.** *Resources, most importantly people, need to be available to leaders for back-up and support as needed.* "Time-outs" tend to be misused for youths and under utilized for staff. Leaders need both permission and a means to remove themselves from the group or interaction with an individual if they feel they are overwhelmed and have exhausted strategies and/or their energies.

In addition to crisis relief, supervisors should take the initiative to give brief, spontaneous breaks to leaders by offering to take a group of youth for a few minutes. This gives the leader a break and significantly improves the image of administration and intra-organizational communication since administration is perceived as accessible and willing to get "in the trenches."

❑ **Identify Special Needs.** *Special needs of youth, in addition to age, should be considered when establishing small groups* in order to prevent any one leader/group from being overburdened with problematic youths or a combination of youths that feed into each others' misbehavior. Individuals need to take caution not to overload their more skilled staff with children who have special needs.

❑ **Develop a Sense of Humor.** *Humor and discipline are not mutually exclusive.* Children are able to take a leader seriously who has an informal rapport and likes to joke around with them at times. The key here for the leader is knowing what times are appropriate for humor and when discipline is dictated. For example, if someone's safety is in jeopardy, it is imperative that a leader has established him/herself as an authority figure that youth will respond to without question.

❑ **Be Aware of Body Language.** *Body language and tone of voice are at least as important as the actual words spoken.* A recent study indicated that the content of what was being said held the smallest percentage of importance in communication with the most important being tone of voice and then body language. The essence of a message can be drastically different depending on the way the message is communicated.

❑ **Validate Feelings.** *Address youth behavior, but validate youth feelings.* The purpose of any discipline strategy is to stop negative behavior and/or elicit positive behavior while maintaining the youth's sense of self-worth. In other words, when in trouble youths should feel they are doing a bad thing rather than that they are a bad person.

Furthermore, it is acceptable for someone to feel angry, but that does not mean that they can physically or verbally attack the person who has made them angry. *People, including children, must learn to control their behavior in spite of certain feelings.*

Likewise, the youth who has a superficial injury and is crying as though they are in need of emergency treatment is not reassured by a leader saying: "You're OK. It doesn't hurt." While it may be that they are overreacting to the injury, they are feeling hurt and in need of attention. Having their feelings dismissed is the last thing that will help expedite their "recovery" and get them back involved in the program's activities.

❑ **Maintain the Integrity of all Youth.** *Maintain youths' integrity within the group at all times.* Especially with school-age children and adolescents, peers are a very important influence. Whenever possible, negative feedback to youths should take place with discretion so as to protect their place in their peer group at youth center. This will also help eliminate the problem of children looking for negative feedback as a means of impressing their peers. By keeping the interaction between leader and individual youth, the power and potential disruption of the group's influence is minimized.

❑ **Be Honest.** *Admit mistakes and shortcomings as a leader.* When genuine, this elicits respect, not rebellion. Many leaders fall into the trap of feeling they need to be perceived as perfect in order to be in control. Children are perfectly capable of understanding that adults make mistakes and life is not always fair. Seeing the humanity of their leader will actually help the relationship between leader and youths and it is building this relationship that is the most powerful and effective tool in managing youth behavior.

❑ **Develop a Variety of Strategies for Dealing with Youth Behavior.** Seek input and advice from colleagues and administrators before feeling frustrated and overwhelmed. Have a repertoire of behavior management strategies which can easily be implemented at any time. The following list of strategies and principles provide a beginning:

Reinforce positive behavior immediately and consistently;

Ignore undesired behavior;

Reward small, successive steps to desired behavior or skill;

Communicate expectations clearly;

Give adequate attention to avoid extreme attention-seeking behavior;

Do not ignore or tolerate misbehavior when it is harmful or unsafe;

Pick your battles — do not expend a great deal of time or energy in every intervention;

Model desired behavior. Behavior of respected and/or prestigious people is modeled;

Encourage behavior that is incompatible with undesired behavior; and

Adjust reinforcers to meet needs and/or interests of each individual. Competitive events may foster feelings of worthlessness in "losers."

Leaders can begin to become more aware of how they relate to youths by monitoring the self-observation skills listed in the exercise below.

LEADER SELF-HELP EXERCISE

A Leader self-help exercise developed by Robert Ditter, M.Ed., LCSW

This is a list of behaviors (things to do) and ideas (things to think about) that you can use in your dealings with youths. It is not a test. The list is designed to help you do several things, as follows: (1) Be able to begin to watch yourself while you relate to youths; (2) Think about how your dealings with youths are going; (3) Have specific things to practice.

Use a scale from 0 ("never") to 10 ("always") to rate yourself on the following items. A "5" would mean you do this 50% of the time; a "9" would be 90% of the time.

When I talk with youths, I . . .

make eye contact

use touch (like a hand on a shoulder)

kneel down to be on the same physical level when possible

When I am disciplining a youth, I . . .

am clear myself about my goal in discipline (to change behavior; not make the child feel bad)

keep in mind that "I like you; I don't like what you do"

have child maintain eye contact with me

allow a child to tell her story

clearly name what the problem is

clearly name what I expect from the child or what the rules are

ask if the child thinks she can keep the agreement

give clear reasons for rules

admit when I don't know the reason for rules

promise to find out reasons for rules (when I don't know), and follow through

In dealing with youths, I . . .

tend not to feel attacked and am able to keep from taking things personally

make clear the differences between feelings and actions

give permission for feelings, but set firm limits about what is done with them

can commiserate with a youth's feelings (have empathy) and still set rules

am able to enlist the youth in a "partnership" to work on problem solving together

---

USING CONFLICT RESOLUTION TO PROMOTE A PEACEFUL ENVIRONMENT

According to Koch (1992), conflict is a normal part of everyone's lives, and is certainly to be expected in any work involving children. Conflict often occurs between children, between children and their supervisors, and sometimes among the supervisors themselves.

Whomever the disputants are and whatever the cause of the conflict, it is important to recognize that the outcome of the problem depends upon the response. How we respond to conflict is something we can control, and our response will determine not only whether a positive resolution is reached, but what sort of relationship we will have with the disputant(s) in the future.

The term conflict resolution refers to a process — that is a series of steps — which helps people who disagree about something to find solutions that are agreeable to both parties. The idea behind conflict resolution is to create solutions where both disputants feel that they have gained something — where both disputants win. This section of the program guide offers basic guidelines for addressing conflict in a youth service setting and provides a step-by-step process that children and adults can use to resolve their own conflicts or to assist others in creative conflict resolution.

Basic Guidelines for Conflict Resolution in the Youth Service Setting

Regardless of the individuals involved or the nature of the conflict, the following guidelines are important for establishing an environment where healthy, positive conflict resolution is the norm (Koch, 1992).

1.   Make a commitment to prevention.

2.   Be consistent.

3.   Be a model.

4.   Respect others.

What To Do When Conflict Occurs

When conflict occurs, the **response** of individuals to the conflict event will determine whether the situation gets better or gets worse. Certain actions will almost always escalate conflict and other particular actions will almost always decrease the intensity of the problem. According to Koch (1992), some important ways to de-escalate conflict and increase the likelihood of a positive solution, whether you are a disputant or a third-party conflict manager, are:

1.   **Speak in a normal tone.** Shouting is almost a guaranteed escalator of conflict, because the other disputant

will either feel the need to match your tone in order to be heard or s/he will be so offended or intimidated that no further communication will be offered.

2. **Sit Down.** Particularly when dealing with children, the simple act of sitting down rather than standing up sends a message of concern and conciliation. Sitting down says you are willing to give up some power and listen. (It is also much more difficult to be angry and shout from a seated position.)

3. **Allow physical space.** When two people are in conflict, physical separation of at least a few feet means safety . Physical closeness often means intimidation.

4. **Allow time to cool off if needed.** If emotions are intense, a brief cooling-off period can prevent violence and/or inappropriate statements or expressions of emotion. If individuals involved in a dispute cannot carry on a rational discussion of the problem, they probably need a little time to cool off. (With children, only a few minutes may be required.)

5. **Eliminate toxic language.** Name-calling and using offensive language usually increases conflict.

6. **Acknowledge and express feelings openly and appropriately.** It is important for people who disagree to share their feelings. This allows the listener to better understand their view of the problem. The phrase "I feel" followed by a named emotion is a simple way to share feelings without escalating the problem.

7. **Listen carefully and actively.** Active listening means that we show our interest through nonverbal behaviors (facial expression, eye contact, posture), as well as by asking encouraging and clarifying questions, eliminating interruptions, and restating what has been said.

8. **Use a conflict-resolution process** to assist in finding a creative and acceptable solution.

Finding Creative Solutions to Conflicts

The following conflict resolution process is a creative and positive way to resolve problems that typically arise in the youth service environment. This four-step process, which includes establishing ground rules, defining the problem, finding solutions, and follow-up, can be taught to children and adults as a process for problem solving **without a third-party mediator.**

---

2 X 4
Eight Minutes to Conflict Resolution for Youth

The following process is a quick and positive way to resolve relatively simple problems that have not been simmering for a long period of time, between a leader and a child, *or* between two children. The following ground rules apply:

1.   Both disputants agree to work to solve the problem.
2.   Disputants must speak honestly.
3.   There can be no interrupting, name-calling or physical violence.
4.   Discussion must focus only on the issue at hand.

To begin the 2 X 4 process, one disputant requests a few minutes of the other disputant's time to discuss a problem. Children can be taught this process by the youth leader and, thereby, solve simple problems themselves.

2 MINUTES	**STEP 1:**	Disputant #1 states the problem -what has happened and how she/he feels about it. (I feel . . . when you . . . because).
		For example, "<u>I feel</u> angry *when you* call me names *because* it hurts my feelings."
2 MINUTES	**STEP 2:**	Disputant #2 follows the same process.
2 MINUTES	**STEP 3:**	SILENCE— Each disputant spends two minutes thinking about what he/

she can do to solve the problem. (Hmmmmm ... what can I do to solve this problem?)

2 MINUTES   **STEP 4:**   Disputants share the ideas they have thought of and decide what each is willing to do.

Source: Koch, S. (1992). Cedar Falls, IA: University of Northern Iowa.

When children see and use creative and peaceful conflict resolution strategies, they learn that cooperation is better than competition; that their own needs can be met without sacrificing the needs of others, and that they are capable of resolving their own problems without resorting to violence.

HOW TO HANDLE YOUTH WITH SPECIAL NEEDS

Each program needs to have a pre-determined criteria of what special needs they can handle within their youth program. While having youths with disabilities or behavior problems can enrich a program, no one is served if the youth center is not able to adequately meet the special needs of these youths. According to DeGraaf andDeGraaf, such special needs may include:

❑ **History of severe behavioral maladjustment** such as running away, violence, fire setting or previous diagnosis of a psychological disorder (autism, psychosis, attention deficit disorder [hyperactive], schizophrenia, etc.).

❑ **Medical problems** such as asthma, epilepsy, hyperactivity, HIV infected / AIDS.

❑ **Developmental delay** or condition such as learning disorder / mental retardation, attention deficit disorder, etc.

❑ **Communication problems** such as speech disorder, hearing impairment, language barrier.

Criteria to be reviewed regarding program considerations for youth with special needs as cited by DeGraaf and DeGraaf (1994), includes the following.

✓ **What is the staff/youth ratio?** Is adequate staff supervision available to ensure the safety of all participants? Are administrators and/or support staff available to provide one-on-one intervention if needed?

✓ **What are the physical facilities available?** Can a youth who uses a wheelchair navigate at the youth center given its degree of accessibility?

✓ **How much access is there to resource people** such as leisure services staff, volunteers and other youths who can help provide assistance to the youth with special needs? If there is no one available, can a family member of the youth with special needs be utilized to supplement the regular staff?

✓ **What are the necessary qualifications and specialized training needed for staff?** Is someone available (youth, staff or volunteer) to interpret to a youth who does not speak the primary language in case of emergency? Are staff physically capable of moving the youth with special needs, if the child should need assistance?

✓ **What is the program's impact upon the youth?** Will the youth be able to participate in the program to an extent that will be beneficial?

✓ **Is the medical problem controlled** with medication which can be appropriately controlled and dispensed at the youth center? Is a registered nurse necessary and if so, is one available on the grounds at all times? Are emergency procedures in place to deal with problems should they become severe?

✓ **Does the age and size of the youth allow for flexibility in group placement?** For example, can a youth with a developmental delay be physically incorporated into a younger group more consistent with their capabilities?

HELPING YOUTH FEEL VALUED

One of the key ingredients in effective program implementation and excellence in customer service is to include something in a program, activity or event that makes youth feel that they received more than they anticipated and that they are "valued."

There are leaders who provide basic services — no more, no less — and then there are those leaders who "add in" items to their service that *tell youth "we value you, we care about you, we want to do something extra for you, we want to do something special for you."*

The idea of "adding" something extra to the basic services that youth leaders provide, is called the "value added" concept. There are a number of items and services that can be added to programs, activities and events, including special features, level of excellence and youth/leader connection to make youth feel valued.

❑   Adding Special Features

❑   Providing Excellence

❑   Giving Personal Attention

❑   Structuring the Surroundings

❑   Exceeding Anticipated Value

Adding Special Features

Special features can be added to any program, activity or event that make it better than youth expect it to be and tell them they are valued. *When a youth leader takes the time to plan and organize special features, it tells youth that they are important and special.*

For example, at one event for youth, one group of youth leaders spent a weekend transforming their facility into a malt shop with wall murals, a jukebox and decorations. They wore 1950s costumes and set up the "malt shop" with different types of ice cream and toppings for sundaes. One little boy came in and said, "Is this really *all for me?*" Adding such special features makes youth feel important and valued.

Promoting Excellence

Another thing that tells youth that they are valued is the level of excellence of programs, activities and services. *A high level of excellence and planning says that the youth leader cared enough to put time and effort into programs,* activities and services so that youth would have a good experience.

Giving Personal Attention

Personal *attention indicates to youth that the leader cares about them and that they are valued as individuals.* Greeting youth by name as they come in the door, and then thanking them as they leave, remembering what is important to them, making eye contact, are ways that the youth leader can tell youth "you are important, I value you." *Giving praise honestly, yet freely* is another way to make youth feel valued. Reinforcing positive behavior will not only make youth feel valued, but will lead to more of such behavior in the future. Certificates can be given to any youth to say "You're the greatest!" "You're a Rising Superstar!"

Keeping the Facility Clean/Organized

The way in which a facility is maintained, in terms of order and cleanliness will also send a message to youth. It says, *we care enough about you to make the environment you come into a nice place to be.* No one, including youth, want to spend time in a cluttered, disorganized and dirty environment.

Exceeding Anticipated Value

Even though youth may not spend money to participate in many of the services provided by youth leaders, they do spend their time and they deserve to receive a positive return on that investment of time. When *youth feel that they receive more than they anticipated for their investment of time and energy* they will not only feel valued, but they will build commitment and loyalty to the youth leader and the organization.

Spending Time

There are a number of methods that the youth leader can use to make youth feel valued. Probably the most important thing underlying all of these is *the leader's willingness to care enough to devote time.* In order to make youth feel valued, the youth leader will need to devote time to planning, to creating special items for youth, to keeping the facility clean and organized and to giving youth the personal attention they need.

PROMOTING YOUTH LEADERSHIP AND OWNERSHIP

An important job of the youth leader is the incorporation of youth in the planning and implementation processes. How does the leader initiate youth leadership? Youth involvement? Youth ownership? There are a number of advantages to involving youth in programming.

Put yourself in their place... Would you want someone else planning all of your leisure activities so that all you do is show up and participate? Or, do you prefer to have some input in how you spend your time? Youth also have ideas about how they want to spend their time and by being involved in the planning and implementation processes, they can influence the planning process toward their needs. The leader can interact with youths in ways which will foster a sense of ownership. This can be assisted by providing:

❑ **Choice.** Opportunities for youth to choose between several program options.

❑ **Flexibility.** Program flexibility to make adjustments in the schedule based on youth inputs and needs.

❑ **Autonomy.** Providing for opportunities for self-direction within activities. For example allowing youths to develop their own skit which may deviate from what staff envisioned or adapting rules of a game to fit the youths' needs or desires.

❑ **Progression in Activities.** A progression of skills based on ability, age and/or experience must be incorporated into the program in order to meet the needs of veteran youths. By providing them special opportunities not available to the other youths, youth interest and program diversity is maintained.

Following is a simple step-by-step plan for involving youth in creating, planning and implementing programs. The youth leader encouraging youth involvement acts as a supporter, resource-person, encourager and coach.

❑ **Brainstorming Session.** Have youth participate in a brainstorming session to determine what is important to them and where their interests lie. Using a modified nominal group technique — the leader can ask for as many suggestions as possible from all of the group members, hundreds if possible, until the ideas for activities have been exhausted.
The ideas should be put up on marker board, or sheets of newsprint. And, then, ask that youth vote for their favorite ideas, gradually reducing the number of ideas in the pool, until they reach a consensus that several specific ideas are worth pursuing and have chosen one with which they want to begin.

❑ **Choosing a Strategy.** Have youth develop a strategy for carrying out their idea, including facilities, roles and responsibilities, equipment, materials, outline or schedule of events, publicity, systems for control, anticipated outcomes, time and date of program, step-by-step visualization of the event, and other relevant activities. As the leader, you will need to assume a role of resource person, offering needed information but allowing youth to make their own decisions.

❑ **Implementation.** Provide sufficient support to ensure that the program is carried out successfully, while allowing the youth to take control over their activity. Give young people sufficient guidance to *ensure* that they are highly successful. Give them freedom to carry out the project themselves, but not so much freedom that they fail because you don't intervene with information and corrective guidance.

❑   **Evaluation.** The program should offer a learning experience for youth; providing an opportunity to discuss what went right, what went wrong and what would be done differently next time. It is important that you give encouragement and support to youth and that they have a feeling of accomplishment.

❑   **Wrap-Up.** Youth need opportunity to reflect on their accomplishments.   An informal meeting that rewards them for their participation with an item of recognition (such as a certificate or t-shirt) or refreshments, allows them to reflect on their efforts and begin to discuss new activities. This can provide positive reinforcement from both leaders and peers.

HANDLING CUSTOMER COMPLAINTS

Fast and effective resolution of customer complaints *will not only solve the problem at hand, but will maintain customer loyalty.* The customer (youth, parent, community) will tell others about the positive action by your organization if you handle complaints quickly and professionally. In fact, if the leader handles complaints quickly it may actually improve the image of the organization. This discussion provides information to help you handle customer complaints:

❑   Customer Complaint Profile

❑   Customer Complaint Action Plan

❑   Customer Complaint Input

Customer Complaint Profile

Customer complaints are very important, because each complaint received may represent a number of individuals who feel the same way, but don't take the trouble to actually lodge a formal complaint. Studies conducted by "Technical Assistance Research Programs, Inc." for the White House Office for Consumer Affairs found the following.

- ❑   The average business *never hears from 96 percent of its unhappy customers.* For every complaint received, the average organization in fact has *26 customers with problems,* 6 of which are serious problems.

- ❑   Complainers are *more likely than non-complainers to do business again with the company that upset them,* even if the problem isn't satisfactorily resolved.

- ❑   Of the customers who register a complaint, between 54 and 70 percent will do business again with the organization if their complaint is resolved. That figure goes up to *a staggering 95 percent if the customer feels that the complaint was resolved quickly.*

- ❑   The average customer who has had a problem with an organization tells 9 or 10 people about it. Thirteen percent of people who have a problem with an organization *recount the incident to more than 20 people.*

- ❑   Customers who have complained to an organization and had their complaints satisfactorily resolved, *tell an average of five people about the treatment they received* (Albrecht and Zemke, 1985:6).

What does this mean in terms of your organization? It means that if you have a complaint from a parent, a child, an administrator or officer, and you handle it quickly, directly and sensitively, you will minimize the damage caused by the problem and, in fact, may enhance your organization's image.

In handling customer complaints, it is important to *acknowledge the importance of the problem, gather all relevant information before reaching a conclusion, offer a solution and follow through on the commitment you have made* on behalf of your organization.

CUSTOMER COMPLAINT ACTION PLAN

Once a customer complaint has been acknowledged it then becomes important to take the proper corrective steps and actions necessary to resolve the complaint. Dealing effectively with complaints means understanding and responding to the important elements from the customer's point of view.

The expectations of the customer are that something will effectively be changed or solved. The following outlined steps demonstrate the course of action that can be taken to deal with a customer complaint.

❑   **Acknowledge to the Customer the Importance of His/Her Complaint Immediately**

Customer complaints must be taken seriously. *If a customer feels strongly enough about confronting the staff about a problem it is best to be supportive, positive and take a problem-solving orientation.* **Involve the customer** in gathering relevant information and identifying correctable problem solving options. Hold yourself and the organization accountable for the problem.

❑   **Gather Information from the Staff and Other Sources about the Complaint**

Seek out more specific answers about the complaint immediately. *Don't be selective about obtaining information, listen for problem-related cues from both the staffs and the customers point of view.* In order to uncover precisely what the problem is it may be necessary to ask questions like, "what happened, when, why and with whom?"

❑   **Develop and Carry Out a Plan of Action**

Once all the information has been gathered it is then possible to *develop a plan of action* necessary to respond to the complaint, with the input of your supervisor. Individuals within the organization should be willing to bend to meet the needs of customers.

❑   **Follow-Up**

Careful attention must be taken to ensure that commitments and promises made to customers are kept. It may be appropriate to follow-up with the customer at a later date to make sure that the complaint was resolved satisfactorily.

❑   **Review the Organization's Commitments to Customer Service**

No customer complaint is too small or too insignificant to be discounted. *Customer commitment should be clearly stated and confirmed daily* by the organization and staff. A broken promise to one customer is a broken promise to the ideals of customer service.
Even when things may have gone wrong, the ability to deal with complaints effectively can impact very dramatically on the success of the organization.

Leaders should *operate with straightforward sincerity, supportive and helping friendliness, and generous courtesy.* By exhibiting these behaviors leaders can promote a positive and supportive relationship with customers.

Customer Input

Although the youth leader can request input from customers (youth/parents/ community) personally, it is also a good idea to have available *a formal system for receiving customer input, in the form of customer suggestion or complaint cards* placed at programs, activities and events. The leader must get as much feedback from customers as possible in order to identify strengths and problem areas. Customer input/suggestion cards offer a non-confrontational method for giving input.

Action Plan Steps in Handling Customer Complaints

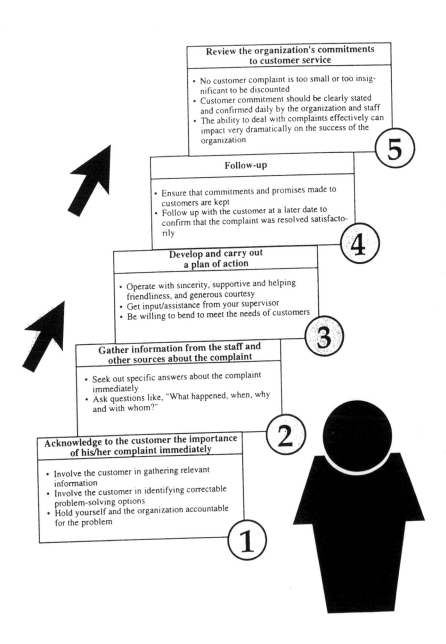

Review the organization's commitments to customer service

- No customer complaint is too small or too insignificant to be discounted
- Customer commitment should be clearly stated and confirmed daily by the organization and staff
- The ability to deal with complaints effectively can impact very dramatically on the success of the organization

5

Follow-up

- Ensure that commitments and promises made to customers are kept
- Follow up with the customer at a later date to confirm that the complaint was resolved satisfactorily

4

Develop and carry out a plan of action

- Operate with sincerity, supportive and helping friendliness, and generous courtesy
- Get input/assistance from your supervisor
- Be willing to bend to meet the needs of customers

3

Gather information from the staff and other sources about the complaint

- Seek out specific answers about the complaint immediately
- Ask questions like, "What happened, when, why and with whom?"

2

Acknowledge to the customer the importance of his/her complaint immediately

- Involve the customer in gathering relevant information
- Involve the customer in identifying correctable problem-solving options
- Hold yourself and the organization accountable for the problem

1

LIABILITY CONCERNS, RISK MANAGEMENT PLANS AND PROCEDURES

Providing a safe experience for youth should be the number one priority of all staff. Such a goal requires constant attention to detail and the "what if's" of a youth program. This process is often referred to as risk management. *A risk is an uncertainty or probability concerning the loss of resources.* In a camp setting these resources may be individual youth or staff members, or the facility itself.

In order for the youth leader to truly understand the risk management process, the following terms and concepts need to be reviewed.

❑ **Risk Management Plans.** It is important for staff to develop ways to manage risk associated with programs. *A risk management plan is a tool for identifying and controlling the risk or hazards while maximizing the camps' effectiveness with youth.* The objectives of a risk management plan are threefold. First, to provide a safe environment for youth and staff. Second, to anticipate potential hazards and problem situations and plan for them. Third, to provide a plan to follow in crisis situations, thus protecting staff and the program from accusations of negligence.

❑ **Negligence.** In order to prove negligence, four elements must exist.

> **Duty Owed.** There must be duty owed by the person in charge to the participant or staff member. The duty owed by a youth center is to provide a safe environment.

> **Breach of Duty.** There must be breach of duty that results in an accident. Defense on this point would be to show that the staff member did everything he or she could do based on the current body of knowledge and that all appropriate

emergency procedures were followed. Therefore the accident was an unforeseeable event that was not a breach of duty. This brings out the importance of staff training and documentation of such training as well as being able to show well-thought-out emergency procedures.

Resulting Accident. The breach of duty must be directly responsible for the accident.

Actual Damage Incurred. There must be actual damage or loss sustained as a result of the injury.

❐ **Standard of Care.** When asked to decide if a staff member is negligent in a certain situation the courts will compare the action of the staff member to a reasonably prudent person. *For youth leaders, the courts will hold them to the level of care of a professional, college-educated youth leader.* The actual way that appropriate behavior is most commonly judged by the courts is through the opinions of experts in the field, the written standards of the profession, or both.

The key people in developing and implementing a risk management plan are the youth leader and other front line staff. Having the youth leader involved in the creation and practice of risk management plans helps staff feel ownership of these plans as well as realize the need for everyone to be involved in making a safe environment. Leaders must develop a frame of mind which constantly anticipates potential dangers and deals with them effectively. In such a mindset, leaders should be aware of the environment and equipment, the staff involved, and the participants.

Suggested Risk Management Procedures

In developing a risk management plan, the youth leader needs to follow a five-step process:

❑ **Identify risks/potential hazards.** Define what constitutes a crisis in one's particular facility or area as well as identify how to deal with special circumstances when they arise. Three areas that are potential risk areas are staff, activities and participants.

❑ **Evaluate risks/potential hazards.** Evaluate risks/hazards in terms of potential impact and imminence.

❑ **Select the most appropriate method for handling each risk.** Choices for dealing with risks include: *avoiding risks* in situations that happen frequently and have severe consequences, *retaining and reducing risks* in situations that happen frequently but are not severe (i.e. skinned knees) or are neither frequent nor severe, and *transferring risks*, through insurance, in situations that have severe consequences, but rarely happen. In addition to selecting the most appropriate method for handling the risk, risk management plans should also:

> **Be Action Oriented.** Specify specific actions to be taken immediately by specific individuals.
>
> **Clarify Communication.** Lines of communication should be clear and distinct to alleviate any possible confusion about who needs to be told what and who needs to do what.
>
> **Follow-up Procedures.** Once the initial crisis is past, staff must still deal with the aftermath of the crisis. As a result, someone should be designated the crisis manager and another person should deal with the media. All events need to documented by the leader(s) involved in the incident. All tasks should be designated to specific individuals in writing within the risk management plan.

❑ **Implement the Plan.** Plans need to be discussed and practiced during staff trainings so each person knows what is expected of them. Role play emergencies throughout training to practice emergency procedures.

❑ **Review the Plan**. Periodic reviews of risk management plans are essential to keep them up to date with current industry standards. Legal counsel should be sought to review plans periodically along with other professionals within the youth services field.

Special situations which require a risk management plan include: fires, motor vehicle accidents, near drownings, medical emergencies, severe storms (i.e. tornados, flash floods), death of a staff member, death of a youth, missing youth, child abuse, boating accidents, lightning strikes, strangers in the area and other accidents. This is not an all- inclusive list! Leaders and other staff must identify all potential risks at their particular site and develop a risk management plan which addresses their unique situation and staff.

RISK MANAGEMENT QUIZ

Following is a brief quiz designed to provoke thought regarding some aspects of risk management. Adapted from Jordan (1992), it is not comprehensive but is intended to be a tool to encourage you, as a youth leader, to seek out additional information about your role in risk management.

1. Explain and define to what standard of care you will be held accountable during programs (level of care that is expected of you by law).

    Will be held to the level of a professional, college-educated, youth leader. To the same standards as a trained leader in a similar situation as a parent.

2. Explain the type of supervision required for the following activities. Also explain *why* you need that type of supervision.

    Swimming: *Specific when teaching; close general when recreational swim. Know hazards of water areas.*

Arts and crafts: *General. Low level of risk, controlled activity. If young children and scissors, closer supervision required.*

Nature hike: *General. Low risk, leaders must maintain general group control.*

Large group games: *General. Low risk, nature of the activity must be considered. Must follow progression, sequencing is important.*

Small group games: *General. Low risk, nature of the activity must be considered. Must follow progression, sequencing is important.*

Field trips: *General. Consider obvious, familiar risks to youth. Must maintain group control.*

3.   Why is it important to teach or lead games and activities in a progression?

*If progression teaching is not followed, children might be pushed into something for which they are not prepared (emotionally, physically, psychologically). The counselor has a responsibility to insure that youth are prepared for the activity, and **must have observed that the child is ready.** Failure to observe or have proof of such readiness can put the leader in a compromising situation.*

4.   As a professional working with children you will be expected to be aware of the three main risk management components; identify those components.

1. the environment   2. the staff   3. the participants

5.   Why is it important for you to be aware of the moods and fatigue levels of your fellow staff members?

To be able to adjust to the needs of staff. Moods and fatigue can interfere with one's judgment and ability to lead in a safe manner. Over tired staff, or staff in a bad mood, will need extra assistance and reminders to stay safe and alert.

6. You notice a fellow staff member leading an activity in an unsafe fashion. *What* do you do and *when* do you do it?

   Stop them in a tactful fashion and correct the problem. Do it immediately!

7. What should you do *every* day before activities begin to minimize risk?

   Do a visual check of the grounds, equipment, and facilities. Check in with staff to ascertain needs.

RISK MANAGEMENT: HOW MUCH DO YOU KNOW?

This questionnaire developed by Jordan (1992) will assess your current knowledge of risk management and help you further assess your own information needs. For each of the following items place a T if the item is true, an F if the item is false.

1. F   Risk management means the same thing as liability. (*no, responsibility*)

2. F   You can assume that facilities will be safe. (*false*)

3. T   If a child gets hurt, you can be sued no matter whose fault it is. (*can get sued for anything, anytime*)

4. F   Once a child and parent/guardian signs an activity waiver, they cannot sue you if the child gets injured. (*waivers are just to make people think; you cannot sign away your right to sue others*)

5. F   The type of supervision needed for every recreational activity is the same as other activities. (*some need general, some need specific*)

6. F   You can't get sued if you don't have any money. (*anyone can get sued, your wages can be garnisheed*)

7. F   As a youth leader, your standard of care is less than that of

the child's parents. (*standard of care is greater than parents*)

8. F   As long as you warn participants it is okay to play on a slippery surface. (*never play in hazardous areas*)

9. F   Legally, a child under the age of 14 is considered to not understand basic hazards. (*child under 12 is considered not to understand*)

10. F   A child has not yet been picked up by their parents and your shift is over; you are no longer responsible for that child. (*you are responsible until another authorized adult relieves you*)

11. F   There does not need to be an injury for you to be held liable. (*must have duty, breach of duty, proximate cause, injury*)

12. F   As a leader, you are only responsible for open and obvious hazards. (*you are responsible for knowing about hidden hazards as well*)

13. F   If a child gets injured and other children's parents want to know what happened, you should tell them. (*only the Program Director should inform parents. You could be liable for providing misinformation, and you could make a bad situation worse*)

14. F   You cannot be held liable if a child hurts another child. (*you are responsible for the care and protection of children from all hazards*)

15. F   The most dangerous activity you will engage in is aquatics. (*transportation*)

16. F   If a young participant is hurt while horsing around, you cannot be held responsible for that. (*you are responsible for the care and protection of children from all hazards*)

17. T   As a leader you will be expected to know all the potential hazards of an activity. (*true*)

18. T   Recreation leaders are responsible for the condition and use of equipment in programs. (*true*)

19. T   Prevention is the best risk management plan you can have. (*true*)

20. T   To be liable for something is to be responsible for it. (*true*)

RISK MANAGEMENT CHECKLIST

Facility/Structure

_____ Are the lights in working order throughout the facility?

_____ Is the floor clear of debris (paper, trash, broken glass, dirt, etc)?

_____ Is the floor clear of water?

_____ Are obstacles clear from the play area (unused equipment, tables, chairs, etc)?

_____ Do you have a clear view of all playing areas?

_____ Is the area secure from unauthorized visitors?

_____ Does the structure have any inherent hazards (exposed bolts, splinters, rough surfaces, etc)?

_____ Where is this facility in relation to potential danger zones (roads, water, etc)?

_____ Are the facilities appropriate for the weather conditions?

_____ Is the facility clean?

_____ Is the structure in good working order?

_____ Where is the nearest emergency telephone?

_____ Is there indoor access in case of inclement weather (humidity, lightning, etc)?

Grounds

_____ Is the ground surface smooth and free from holes and divets?

_____ Is the ground clear of debris (paper, trash, broken glass, dirt, etc)?

_____ Is the ground clear of water?

_____ Is the ground surface slippery?

_____ Is the ground the appropriate surface for this activity?

_____ If playing at dusk or dark, is the area well lit?

_____ Do you have a clear view of all playing areas?

_____ Is the area secure from unauthorized visitors?

_____ Where are these grounds in relation to potential danger zones (roads, water, etc)?

_____ Where is the nearest emergency telephone?

Equipment

_____ Is the equipment in good working condition?

_____ Is the equipment being used as it was intended?

_____ Is the equipment appropriate for this activity and age group?

_____ Does this equipment have inherent hazards (i.e. earth ball, scuba gear)?

_____ Is it possible that this equipment will break in the middle of an activity?

_____ What are the possible misuses of this equipment?

———— Is it appropriate for participants to play on/with this equipment
———— unsupervised?
———— Is a first aid kit available?
———— Is water available?

CHILD ABUSE

Child abuse takes many forms and includes physical abuse, emotional/verbal abuse, sexual abuse and neglect. With statistics indicating that child abuse occurs at what could be considered epidemic proportions (e.g. estimates indicate that 60% of girls and 30% of boys are victims of *sexual abuse*), the number of youth and staff affected by this phenomena is high (DeGraaf and DeGraaf 1994). It is the responsibility of the administrator(s) to develop policies and procedures as well as educate and prepare staff for handling all three of these situations appropriately should they arise.

Youth as Victims of Child Abuse. It is important that staff understand the signs and symptoms of children who are abused. This will help them deal with problematic behavior that occurs as well as identify children who are unknown victims. Research has often proved to be inconclusive, and though children must be individualized, some general patterns are indicated. Youth leaders should also realize how a history of abuse may manifest itself in youth, particularly how they relate to other youth and counselors.

Family Characteristics. Child abuse knows no boundaries and is prevalent in all socioeconomic strata of society; the following factors place families at higher risk.

❑ Parents were deprived of emotional support/ nurturing during childhood
❑ Parents are isolated, lack support systems, and have low self-esteem
❑ Parents have been physically and socially abused
❑ Children have special needs and require extra attention
❑ Parents have learned to discipline only through physical punishment
❑ Parents experience problems in their marital relationship
❑ Families experience some kind of stress (finan-

Characteristics of Abused Children. It is difficult to determine whether characteristics of abused children place them at higher risk to be abused or are the result of abuse. Regardless, the following characteristics can prove helpful in identifying abuse victims.

- Listless, apathetic, unresponsive depressed, shy
- Fearful of physical contact, physical punishment
- May respond negatively to praise
- Reluctant to engage in messy activities
- Preoccupation with bowel movements and/or constipation
- Initially seems to lack the normal childlike sense of joy
- Displays hyperactive, aggressive, compulsive, attention-seeking behavior
- Demonstrates low self-esteem
- Experiences learning problems in school
- Lies about the origin of bruises, burns or other physical injuries
- Has nightmares or talks about abuse in sleep

Policies and Procedures Related to Suspected Child Abuse. All suspicions and actions should remain confidential and only be discussed with the appropriate persons involved.

Step 1: Leaders who have any suspicions of a youth being a victim of child abuse should report that suspicion immediately to a supervisor.

Step 2: The supervisor should contact the organization's director to relay the information.

Step 3: This person determines if more information needs to be gathered, but in most cases a designated person who is trained to talk to a child about such matters and contact the parents is contacted.

Step 4: The leader should file an incident report documenting what happened and how the situation was handled. The leader as well as the supervisor and director should document all their actions during the incident.

Accusations against staff/youth. One of the most difficult challenges for administrators is preventing incidents of abuse by a staff member or other youth and dealing with accusations made by youth and/or their parents. This issue is emotionally laden for all involved, and it is the administrator's responsibility to remain objective, protect the rights of all parties involved (including the accused youth or staff member), and be an advocate for the potential victim by seriously dealing with all allegations.

Policies and Procedures Related to Suspected Child Abuse

Step 1   Staff should never be alone with a youth, especially in a secluded area (e.g. locker rooms, etc). Another staff member should be present to prevent abuse but also to serve as witnesses should an allegation be made. This is important protection for staff and the inconvenience of adhering to this is far outweighed by the benefits.

Step 2   Staff should receive ample training on how to handle youth with special needs and administrative support provided.

Step 3   Youth should never be left unsupervised, especially in secluded areas (e.g. locker rooms, etc).

Step 4   The alleged perpetrator should be removed from the youth group until the allegation can be investigated and evaluated by the designated administrator. Staff should be informed during staff training that this is standard operating procedure and not an indication of presumed guilt on their part. Once exonerated, the staff member/youth should resume their role in group.

Step 5   The youth leader should file an incident report with the organization's director documenting what happened and how the situation was handled.The organization's director should add all his/her actions during the incident.

REPORTS

It is important to document all problems or accidents which may arise. Accident reports, staff journals and incident reports can assist the youth leader in this process.

- **Accident Report.** This form should be filled out any time first aid is applied (including cleaning and/or application of a band-aid for a simple cut or scrape). Copies of all accident reports should be submitted to the organization's director and should be filed and kept for several years. It is a good policy to call the parent whenever an accident has happened (no matter how small) and tell them what happened and the treatment administered.

- **Incident Report.** This form should be filled out to document any incident that takes place. Incidents are any situations that are out of the ordinary during youth programs and include such things as missing youth, suspected child abuse, fighting, thefts, etc. As with accident reports all incident reports should be submitted to the organization's director and should be kept on file for several years.

- **Staff Journals.** Accident and incident reports can be incorporated into some kind of youth center journal where staff keep a running dialogue of what is happening each day. Such a journal can be used to record such things as when medications are given out, when a youth is picked up early, when certain youth are having behavior problems, reminders to staff, etc.

Each of these tools allow staff to document day-to-day operations. *They need to be kept up to date as well as be accurate and precise.* Staff never know when such records may be needed to demonstrate that youth leaders, program staff or administrative acted in an appropriate way during a specific situation.

A Final Note

Although there are a number of procedures, processes, and suggestions related to program implementation, the most important factor related to implementation is helping youth to feel important, to feel a greater sense of self-esteem and to communicate with them through actions and words that they are valued. Youth should always hear more positive things from the leader than negative ones. Even a child with behavior problems is more likely to respond positively over time if the leader tries to "catch" him/her doing something right and offers praise for the behavior on a regular basis.

Personal Notes:
Program Implementation

What are ten attributes of good customer service?

a)   f)
b)   g)
c)   h)
d)   i)
e)   j)

Why is just one customer complaint important? What may one customer complaint represent?

What are four (4) factors that you should consider in terms of risk management?

What are some of the actions that the leader can take to help youth feel valued?

What are techniques that you can use in the area of behavior management with youth?

References

Albrecht, K. and R. Zemke. (1985). Service America! Homewood, IL: Dow Jones-Irwin.

Brandwein, M. (1989).The Eight Great "ates." Presentation at American Camping Association National Conference, Seattle, WA.

Chenery, M. (April, 1985). "Toward a More Concrete Understanding of Child Behavior." *Camping Magazine.*

DeGraaf, D. and K. DeGraaf. (1994). *U.S. Army Youth Services Training Guide: Planning and Supervising Camp Programs* (in press).

Ditter, R. (1988). "Today's Child—Tomorrow's Camp." *Camping Magazine..*

Edginton, C.R. and P.F. Ford. (1985). *Leadership in Recreation and Leisure Service Organizations.* New York: John Wiley & Sons.

Jordan, D. (1992). *Risk Management Guidelines.* Cedar Falls, IA: University of Northern Iowa.

Koch, S. (1992). *Using Conflict Resolution to Promote a Peaceful Environment.* Cedar Falls, IA: University of Northern Iowa.

Lewin, K., R. Lippitt, and R. White. (1939). "Patterns of Aggressive Behavior in Experimentally Created Social Climates." *Journal of Social Psychology.*

Technical Assistance Research Programs, Inc. White House Office for Consumer Affairs, Washington,D.C. (1985). In Albrecht, K. and R.Zemke, *Service America!* Homewood, IL: Dow Jones-Irwin.

CHAPTER 15

Program Evaluation

As a youth leader, you will be responsible for evaluating program services. This chapter of the book offers information regarding the sixth step of the program-planning process — Program Evaluation. Program evaluation is used to help determine how a program impacted the customer, the organization and the degree to which the program was effectively managed. Some of the questions that are asked in the evaluation process are "Did the customer (youth) have a good experience?" "Does the youth exhibit new behaviors as a result of participation in the program?"

Following is the *program evaluation* step as it is presented in the program-planning diagram.

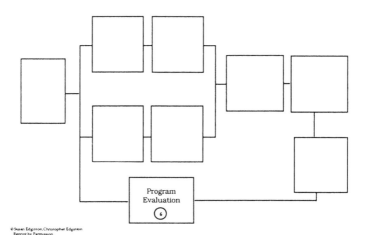

Program Evaluation
(6)

Evaluation is an important part of program planning. It assists in quality control, by measuring how well the leader and the organization achieve the goals and objectives of program(s) by measuring the difference between goals and outcome, expectations and results.

Evaluation should encourage constructive change and growth in a program or organization and may provide information that can be used to justify programs. Some of the activities that take place during this step of the program planning process are:

- Determining Who Should Evaluate

- Determining What Should be Evaluated

- Selecting the Type(s) of Evaluation

- Implementing Methods of Evaluation

Who Should Evaluate?

Anyone who has been affected by, or involved in, the program may, and should, participate in the evaluation process. This includes, youth, their parents, the youth leader, staff, sponsors or others. All of these individuals will have valuable input, and different viewpoints, that will, together, serve to give a more complete picture of the effectiveness of the program, event or service.

What Should Be Evaluated?

The evaluation process attempts to determine how well the goals of the program have been met. This would include the program structure and content, as well as facilities and equipment, site, staff training and effectiveness, publicity, food and other factors.

Evaluation of youth programs is often measured in terms of numbers of participants; that is, a high number of participants is thought to indicate a successful program. However, programs *must be evaluated both in terms of numbers (or statistics) and impact.*

The numbers are important, good attendance at programs and activities is crucial; however, measuring the impact of the program is also of a high degree of importance.

Determining the degree to which the program has impacted on the lives of youth — that is, the skills they have acquired, the values they have incorporated, the changes in their attitudes, the manner in which their behavior has changed and other factors must be observed and measured by the youth leader in order to effectively evaluate a program.

The evaluation process is focused in three different areas, which are:

❑   What has been the outcome for the customer (youth)?

❑   What has been the outcome for the leader?

❑   What has been the outcome for the organization?

Outcome for the Customer (youth/parents/sponsor). Has the behavior of the youth or youths changed as a result of participation as intended? For example, if it was a learning activity, did they learn the skill as specified in performance objectives? Are the participants (youth) satisfied, did they have a good time? Did they feel that their time was spent in a worthwhile manner? Are parents satisfied? What are their reactions and what have their children told them about the program? Are sponsors pleased with the impact of the program as an outcome of their investment of time and/or funds?

Outcome for the Leader. Were the preparations and planning that were undertaken by the leader efficient? Was the program format appropriate, was the leaders' leadership style effective? Was the facility adequate? Were supplies and equipment sufficient? These and other similar types of questions are addressed in this portion of the evaluation process.

Outcome for the Organization. Did the program contribute to the existing goals of the organization as a whole? Did the leader communicate effectively an organizational image that was professional, competent and effective? Are the organization's resources being used effectively in terms of support of the program?

Through effective evaluation processes, the following goals are achieved.

❏   Evaluation helps measure change in customer leisure behavior. It measures the extent to which intended behavior outcomes have occurred.

❏   Evaluation reviews and measures customer satisfaction. The leader may think that customers (youth) are pleased with programs, but evaluation helps to get accurate input from them.

❏   Evaluation provides means by which customers can give input regarding their feelings and attitudes about programs.

❏   Evaluation builds customer support for programs and services. As programs and services are improved, customer loyalty is built. Also customers, feel ownership when they are allowed to have input in the evaluation process.

Types of Evaluation

There are *two major types of evaluation*. The first is ongoing (or formative) evaluation, and the second is the final evaluation (or summative evaluation). The first type of evaluation occurs throughout the program, the second at the end of the program (Edginton et al., 1992). These are briefly described below.

Formative Evaluation. Ongoing, or *formative evaluation* is carried on throughout the program. In other words, the youth leader evaluates the program as it is going on, and then makes corrections necessary to improve the program as it is in process. For example, youth may provide feedback that indicates that the program is not meeting their expectations, at which point the leader may evaluate the situation and restructure the activity. It is important that the leader respond to existing conditions in a flexible manner and not carry out program plans as if they were set in stone.

Summative Evaluation. Final or summative evaluation occurs at the end of the program as a final wrap-up. This type of evaluation attempts to review the entire program, consider its strengths and weaknesses, and then make final judgment on the impact it achieved, the degree to which it met its goals and recommendations for future programs. This process can be carried out in a number of ways.

Not only should the leader conduct an evaluation for each program, but an annual evaluation should be conducted by the leader and organization. The annual evaluation should also make recommendations for the coming year, and be tied into annual comprehensive planning efforts.

Methods of Evaluation

There are a number of specific methods that can be used to evaluate programs and services. Some of these methods are more formal than others. They include verbal response, objective pre- and post-tests, observation, written response and staff evaluations. These are briefly discussed below.

❑   **Verbal response/comments.** This is a very informal approach in which the youth leader simply asks youths for their verbal reaction to the program. Youths can be asked individually, or they can be asked as a group. Their responses can be recorded in writing, or by tape recorder or video. The disadvantage of this approach is that youth may not say what they really think, since they do not have anonymity.

❑   **Objective tests.** The use of pre-and post-tests can be effective in measuring the impact of programs, particularly skill development. In this instance, youth are given some type of test to measure whether or not they have attained knowledge and skills.

This can be done in a "fun" way. For example, skills that the leader has taught in an Adventure Challenge program could be tested in a timed challenge course.

☐   **Observation.** Evaluation through observation is usually done by someone other than the youth leader. An impartial individual, or observer, with knowledge in the youth services area may observe a program and then pass the observations along to the youth leader.

☐   **Written response.** The written response is a commonly used form of evaluation. In this type of evaluation, youth and/or their parents are asked to fill out a rating form to evaluate their experience and to add comments. These rating forms can be made fun with graphics. This type of evaluation is, of course, limited to those who can express themselves in writing. It has been found that youth evaluation forms that require a written comment to each question give valuable information in terms of feelings and impact of the program.

☐   **Staff Evaluation.** The staff (youth leader and others) may fill out their own written program evaluations for record and review. These evaluations may be simple or complex, containing information regarding publicity and promotion, preparations, manpower, activities, and recommendations. A Program Evaluation Summary Worksheet is presented later in this chapter that can help the leader to work though the evaluation process in terms of participation impact, staff impact, costs, perceived success of the program and recommendations.

PROGRAM EVALUATION SUMMARY
WORKSHEET

Program_____ Location _____

Date(s) of Operation _____

Data Summary:

❑   **Participation Impact**
Number of Sessions (NOS)   _____
Number of Enrollments (NOE)   _____
Potential Attendance (PA) = (NOS) x (NOE)   _____
Actual Total Attendance (ATA)   _____
Average Attendance (AVA) = (ATA)/(NOE)   _____
Percentage of Attendance (POA) = (ATA)/(PA)   _____

❑   **Staff**
    Number of Staff (NBS)   _____
    Number of Staff Hours   _____
    Staff/Participant Ratio (SPR) = (AVA)/(NBS)   _____

❑   **Costs**
    Salaries   _____
    Equipment   _____
    Supplies   _____
    Facilities   _____
    Total (TOTC)   _____

❑   **Revenues**
    Organizational Funds or Appropriated Funds
    _____
    User Fees or Nonappropriated Funds
    _____
    Total (TOTR)
    _____

❑   **Cost Analysis**
    Net Cost (TOTC)
    _____
    Average Cost Per Participant (TOTC/NOE)
    _____

Percent Self-Supporting (User Fees/TOTC)

_____

Why was this program conducted? What were the specific goals of this program?

Procedures: Briefly describe what was involved in operating this program.

Evaluation Data:

❑   Program Observations:

❑   Participant Feedback:

Analysis of Evaluation:

What is the program accomplishing?
Who is the program serving?
Is this program the best allocation of these resources?
How does this program compare with other similar programs?
Does this program fit into the organizations goals?

Program Recommendation:

_____ Continued as currently operated
_____ Dropped
_____ Modified as noted below

_____   _____
Signature   Date

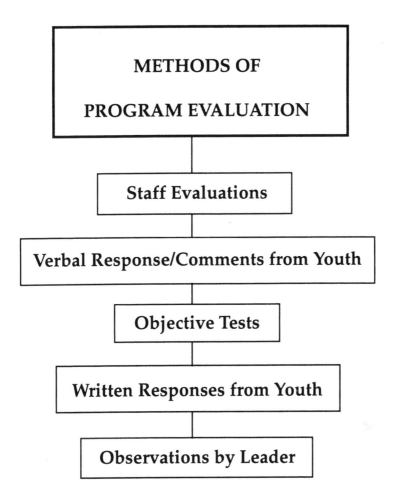

A Final Note

Evaluation does not merely tell the leader whether a program or service was well executed and well received. It offers a mechanism for many types of input and outcomes. Depending upon the type and scope of evaluation, it can offer a means for input from youth, parents, the community, staff, administration and others. In addition, it offers a method for gathering information that can be used to improve services, to be used in promotion, and to facilitate interpersonal communication between staff.

Personal Notes:
Evaluation

What types of questions does an evaluation answer?

_____

_____

_____

Identify five (5) methods of evaluation.

     1.
     2.
     3.
     4.
     5.

What are the two types of evaluation and how are they used?

_____

_____

_____

APPENDIX I

PROGRAM FORMS

ACCIDENT REPORT

Name of injured _____ Age _____

Address of injured _____ Phone _____

Area or Facility _____ Date _____ Time _____

Specific place of accident _____

_____

Description of accident _____

_____

_____

Description of injury or illness _____

_____

_____

Action taken _____

_____

_____

Was the parent contacted ❏ Yes   ❏ No

Was the area where the injury occurred checked ❏ Yes   ❏ No

Action taken _____

Victim's past history of similar injury or illness _____

_____

Witness _____ Phone _____

Address _____

Check Appropriate Phrase

Victim's condition:

   ❏ Conscious with appropriate responses to questions

   ❏ Stuporous or incoherent

   ❏ Unconscious

Breathing:

   ❏ Normal   ❏ Labored   ❏ Rapid/shallow or faint   ❏ Absent

Shock/Illness/Injury Status:

   Skin: ❏ Flushed   ❏ Normal   ❏ Pale   ❏ Clammy

   Eyes (pupils): ❏ Normal and responsive to light   ❏ Dilated   ❏ Unequal size

   Pulse: ❏ Normal   ❏ Rapid, weak   ❏ Slow, pounding

   Facial expression: ❏ Responsive   ❏ Vacant

   Nauseous: ❏ Yes   ❏ No

   Dizzy: ❏ Yes   ❏ No

   Generalized weakness: ❏ Yes   ❏ No

Pain: ❏ Yes   ❏ No

Location and description _____

Distortion/swelling/bruising   ❏ Yes   ❏ No

Location and description: _____

Signed _____ Signed _____

       (Counselor)   (Director)

Place any additional comments on back of this sheet

FIELD TRIP EVALUATION

Theme Week _____   Site _____
Director _____   Date _____
Field Trip to _____

Distance from base: Miles: _____   Travel time: _____
Description of Field Trip Site: _____
_____
_____

Was any advanced preparation undertaken? If so what? _____
_____
_____

Any special concerns regarding field trip site? _____
_____
_____

Overall rating of trip   1   2   3   4   5
                              poor   excellent
Would you recommend this field trip for future summers? ❑ Yes   ❑ No

FIELD TRIP EVALUATION

Theme Week _____   Site _____
Director _____   Date _____
Field Trip to _____

Distance from base: Miles: _____   Travel time: _____
Description of Field Trip Site: _____
_____
_____

Was any advanced preparation undertaken? If so what? _____
_____
_____

Any special concerns regarding field trip site? _____
_____
_____

Overall rating of trip   1   2   3   4   5
                              poor   excellent
Would you recommend this field trip for future summers? ❑ Yes   ❑ No

GENERIC PROGRAM DESIGN GRID

Monday

8:00   Counselor Skit
        _____

8:15   Opening Songs
            Camp Adventure
            Iowa Songs
            Chuggi Chuggi

            _____   _____
            _____   _____
            _____   _____

8:45   Individual Age Groups (IAGs)
            Name Game _____
            Rules _____
            Name Tags _____
            Group Cheer (if Time)

10:15   All Camp Activities
            Game _____
            Game _____
            Game _____

11:30   Lunch

12:00   Structured Free Time
            Mural _____
            _____
            _____

12:30   Rotating Activities   3:30   Closing Activities
                                                 Friends
        Swimming   Penny Song

        _____   _____
        _____   _____

        Sports & Games

        _____
        _____

        Arts & Crafts

        _____
        _____

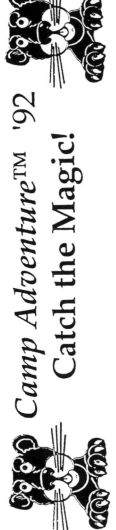

Camp Adventure™ '92
Catch the Magic!

This is to certify that

_____

has met the qualifications for

Camp Adventure Superstar

by showing cooperation, friendship, and enthusiasm. The recipient of this award is eligible to receive the benefits and privileges thereof.

_____   _____
Camp Director   Camp Counselor

_____
Date

INCIDENT REPORT

Location _____   Leader/Staffperson _____

Date _____   Time _____

Youth's Name _____   Address _____

Phone _____   Age _____

Incident (Give complete information and background)

_____

_____

_____

_____

Did any physical or property damage occur? (Give full, specific details)

_____

_____

_____

_____

How was the situation dealt with? _____

_____

_____

What plan does staff have for future to prevent problems or modify behavior?

_____

_____

_____

_____

Signature of Leader

_____

Signature of Supervisor/Director

APPENDIX II

SAMPLE OF WEEKLY
PROGRAM GRID

GENERIC PROGRAM GRID

	Monday	Tuesday	Wednesday	Thursday	Friday
9:00	Daily Welcome • Songs • Drama • Announcements	Daily Welcome • Songs • Drama • Announcements	Daily Welcome • Songs • Drama • Announcements	Daily Welcome • Songs • Drama • Announcements	Daily Welcome • Songs • Drama • Announcements
10:00	Small Group Time • Name Games Make sure everyone knows one another • Initiatives Help the group work together	Clubs • Drama • Arts & Crafts • Nature Activities • Sports & Games	Field Trip Make sure field trips are checked out in advance.	Clubs Encourage a good selection of clubs each week to give campers a variety of choices.	Small Group Time • Special Event Preparation All Camp Activities • Special Event
11:00	All Camp Activities • Active Games	Small Group Time • Low Organized Games	Create a number of bus activities for campers to do in route.	All Camp Activities • Sports	(i.e. carnivals, parades, treasure hunts, etc)
12:00	Lunch & Quiet Time • Low Organized Games	Lunch & Quiet Time • Story Time Read stories to campers. Use the library	Count number of campers both on and off the bus to insure everyone gets back to camp safely.	Lunch & Quiet Time • Board Games	Lunch Make this a special meal to go with the special event
1:30	Clubs Have counselors do commercials to promote clubs	Rotating Activities • Swimming		Rotating Activities Use resources in community	All Camp Swimming
2:30	All Camp Swimming	• Arts & Crafts • Sports & Games	All Camp Swimming	• Bowling • Rollerskating • Swimming	The Big Show Have clubs or small groups present skits, songs, etc.
3:30	Camper's Choice	Camper's Choice	Camper's Choice	Camper's Choice	
4:00	Closing Activities • Songs	Closing Activities • Announcements	Closing Activities • Drama	Closing Activities	Closing Activities • Spirit Stick

TREKIN' IN THE TROPICS

	Tropical Tiki Tour	Cruisin' the Caribbean	Jammin' in the Jungle	River Rampage	Paradise Preservation Parade
9:00	Hello Hot Times	Bon Voyage	Tribal Gathering	Welcome Aboard	Mission Possible
10:00	Parrot Pals	Search Party	W A L K A B O U T	Search Party	Wolfpack
11:00	Colossal Kingdom	Cabin Mates		Slip and Slide	Radical Rainforest Rescue
12:00	Tutti Frutti Treats and Treehouse Time	Fruit Salad and Siesta Surprise		Galley Grub	Animal Crackers
1:30	Search Party	Catch a Wave		Shoot the Rapids	Crystal Springs
2:30	Swimming Hole		Watering Hole		Singin' in the Rain
3:30	Apples or Oranges	Island Madness	Tribal Tricks	Runnin' the Rapids	
4:00	Banana Split	Batton Down the Hatches	Sunset on the Savannah	Bail Out	Homeward Bound

MONDAY
TROPICAL TIKI TOUR

9:00	Hello Hot Times	**Songs:** Camp Theme Song I Like Bananas Nairobi Alligator Song Buzzard Song Junior Birdman	**Weekly Review** **Guidelines of Camp Adventure:** Tarzan comes to camp with Cheeta and friends to explain the laws of the jungle **Spirit Stick:** Groups will be competing for coconuts filled with candy	**Activities:** Announcements: Club Commercials Barnyard Icebreaker to break into small groups Name Tags: Make a passport. Each day check campers in with a different stamp.
10:00	Parrot Pals	**Small Group Time:** Bop Group Juggling Knots Across the Great Divide Balance	During this time make sure everyone in your small group knows everyone's name. Play some of the initiatives listed and then work to come up with a group name and a group cheer. Explain to the group that as they move from activity to activity today they are going to move like different animals (i.e. when the group goes to all camp activities they are going to hop like a kangaroo).	
11:00	Colossal Kingdom	All Camp Activities	**Games:** Four Corners of the World (Four Corners) Giants, Elves, and Wizards Capture the Bird (Capture the Flag)	
12:00	Tutti Frutti Treats	Lunch	**Continuous Activity for the Week** Create five or six animal murals and hide them throughout camp each day. Each animal would have different point totals. Each day small groups would search for the animals. At the end of the week groups would be given points for the animals they found and receive a small prize.	
12:30	Treehouse Time	Quiet time	**Ideas** Younger Campers Get a book from the library and read 2 or 3 chapters each day. Tell the Pink Gorilla Story Older Campers Let campers choose the activities. Suggest a board game tournament.	
1:00	Search Party	Clubs:	**Clubs this week include:** Earthtones, Tropical Tribune, Tracks and Trails Club, Stage Hand Club	**Riddle for the Day** Q: How do you cut an ocean in two? A: With a sea saw
	Swimming Hole	All Camp Swimming		
3:30	Banana Split	Camper Choice	**Daily Spirit Award** Group Spirit will be monitored by monkeys climbing palm trees. The higher the monkey the more group spirit.	**Closing Activity** Have every one stamp their passport by drawing something they liked about today. Place a sticker on each passport as campers leave.
4:00		Songs Alligator Woman Friends		

TUESDAY
CRUISIN' THE CARIBBEAN

9:00 Bon Voyage	**Songs** Camp Theme Song Jamaican Song Princess Pat Rolling over the Billows Down by the Bay	**Welcome Activity** As the group is singing have two counselors act as if they are swabbing the deck of a boat. Have them get into a water fight chasing each other all over the area. Finally one counselor picks up a bucket and corners the other counselor in amongst the campers. The counselor throws the bucket full of confetti paper on all the campers. In addition to this opening skit campers should get into their small groups and update their passports for the day. Do commercials for clubs and choice time.		
10:00 Search Party	**Clubs:** Earthtones: Tropical Tribune: Tracks and Trails Club: Stage Hand Club:	 Continue to work on the group members' paper mache globe. Work continues on the weekly camp newspapers Each day this club tries a new game from the tropics. Today the group is focusing on soccer. Work on the rainforest mural for Friday's Special Event.		
11:00 Cabin Mates	**Small group time** Games: Animal Tag Predator/Prey	Small groups may want to begin to work on their skits for the Friday show. Today small groups may want to imitate swimming from one activity to the next.		
12:00 Fruit Salad	**Lunch**	**Continous Activity Update** Give an update on what animals have been found today and what animals are still lurking about		
12:30 Siesta Surprise	**Quiet Time**	**Ideas** Have campers build boats or rafts out of popsicle sticks. Let them dry and race them on Thursday in a wading pool or running stream. Create an actual regatta and give prizes for best floating boat, best looking boat, fastest boat, etc.		
1:30 Catch A Wave	**Rotating Activities** Swimming Arts and Crafts Games	Play games in the pool, free swim Pine Cone Bird Feeders BVB -- Baseball, Volleyball, Basketball	**Riddle of the Day** Q: What do you get when you cross a parrot with a centipede? A: A walkie talkie	
3:00 Island Madness	**Choice Time**	During the day have a sheet of paper posted where campers can write down activities they would like to play (games, sports, arts and crafts). During this time counselors will offer as many of these activities as they can and campers can choose what they want to do.		
3:30 Batton Down the Hatches **4:00**	**Songs** Row Your Boat Magic Penny	**Daily Spirit Award** Move the monkeys up the tree.	**Closing Activity** Do a commercial for tomorrow's field trip Have each group do their cheer Collect passports	

WEDNESDAY
JAMMIN' IN THE JUNGLE

9:00	**Tribal Gathering**	**Songs** Camp Theme Song Going on a Lion Hunt Crocodile Song I'm Being Swallowed by a Boa Constrictor	**Welcome Activity** Last night one of the counselors fell and hit his head and disa peared thinking he was Tarzan. We think he is in the area an the doctor has told us we need to sing the camp theme song t bring him back to reality. (Male counselor in distance does Tarzan yell and runs off. Campers must catch him and bring back and sing the theme song to him).
10:00	**Walkabout**	**Field Trip** Fun on the Bus **Songs** Wheels on a Bus Who Stole the Cookie Sippin' Cider **Games** Alphabet Game God's Eyes - Make monster eyes Create an add on story about a African Safari. **Idea -- Create a trip box. Include:** Crayons, pencils and paper Library books about the tropics Deck of cards Games for two people (i.e. Battleship) **Field Trip** Trips and Tours Reinforce factors related to risk management when conducting trips and tours. Remember, we guests on our field trips and we must be cognizant of the customs, norms, and values of the culture of those around us. Be careful to maintain control of your group. Some of the principle to follow include: • Counselors will be responsible for a specific number of campers. • Count campers getting on and off the bus -- double check number before leaving location • Get directions to the site well in advance. • Arrange for an interpreter. • Provide information to parents on destination, departure and arrival times, costs, etc. • Obtain signed permission slips. • Be aware of campers' special health considerations. • Establish a meeting place that is easily found if someone gets separated from the group. • Establish meeting times at a site in advance. Scout out field trips in advance (if possible) • Have campers bring a sack lunch and rain gear. • Devise a risk management plan for emergencies which may arise.		
2:30	**Watering Hole**	**Swimming** Games Alligator Tag Ostrich Hunter Duck Under	SWIMMING!!!
3:30 **4:00**	**Sunset on the Savannah**	**Songs** Camper Choice Friends Magic Penny	**Closing Activity** Counselor who was Tarzan has a relapse and runs madly from the gro singing Tarzan of the Apes. Campers must once again catch the couns and sing "Friends" to bring counselor back to reality.

THURSDAY
RIVER RAMPAGE

9:00	Welcome Aboard	**Songs** Camp Theme Song America A boy and girl in a little canoe Fishin' Crawdad	**Welcome Activity** Before campers arrive lay out an obstacle course that campers can track an animal through. Leave little clues along the way. When campers arrive announce to the group that you have seen an animal that is almost extinct in the area. Ask campers to help you track down the animal. Track the animal through obstacle course to an empty nest. Near the nest have a counselor dressed like a river guide with a hose. Spray down the campers and invite them to join counselors on a river rampage today.
10:00	Search Party	**Clubs:** Earthtones: Tropical Tribune: Tracks and Trails Club: Stage Hand Club:	Have group work on creating Fantasea Fish. Talk about what we can do to save coral reefs. Campers should be finishing up their stories, comics, riddles, personals etc as the paper should come out tomorrow in time for the big show. Soccer baseball. Played like baseball except campers can not touch the ball with their hand - must control the ball and kick a goal to get outs. Must work to finish the mural and other decorations for the special event on Friday.
11:00	Slip and Slide	**All Camp Activities** Pictionary	**Games** Create a large Pictionary Board complete with categories involving the Tropics. Play as teams using small groups.
12:00	Galley Grub	**Lunch and Quiet Time**	**Continous Activity Update** Have counselor dressed like a wild animal dash across a nearby field. Campers could try to track the animal down, but don't let animal be caught yet.
1:00	Shoot the Rapids	**Rotating Activities** Arts and Crafts Swimming Camp Regatta	**Ideas** Have everyone work on drawing a flag and costumes for the regatta. Have a parade with an announcer, regatta flags, etc. After the parade have group split in two. One groups swims while the other group races the boats they made on Tuesday. Have boats race two or three at a time.
1:30			**Riddle of the Day** Q: Why did the turtle cross the road? A: To get to the shell station
3:00	Runnin' the Rapids	**Choice Time**	During the day have a sheet of paper posted where campers can write down activities they would like to play (games, sports, arts and crafts). During this time counselors will offer as many of these activities as they can and campers can choose what they want to do.
3:30 4:00	Bail Out	**Songs** Barges Friends	**Daily Spirit Award** Continue to help monkeys climb their palm trees.	**Closing Activity** Have animal be seen again but don't let the animal be caught. Have river guide give out passport stickers today.

FRIDAY
PARADISE PRESERVATION PARADE

9:00	**Mission Possible**	**Songs** Camp Theme Song I Love the Mountains We are the World Skunk Song	**Welcome Activity** Have a mad scientist come running in with the rare animal that campers have been chasing all week. Have the scientist translate how the animal almost became extinct. Include a number of things kids can do to save the planet. Ask campers to help to save the planet. Scientist should proceed to deputize all campers to become environmental rangers. Have campers warm-up by doing the ballet of the air.	
10:00	**Wolfpack**	**Small Group Time** We all need FRIENDS!	**Ideas:** Have campers prepare for the parade celebrating the world in which we live. Campers could dress up as their favorite animals. Make poster to carry which has ideas of what people should do to help the earth. Campers should also plan one booth for the Save the Earth Carnival. Booths might include: face painting, tree planting, environmental trivia, making recycled paper, rainforest mural, fishing for facts, recycling the garbage from camp, making animal puppets, etc.	
11:00	**Radical Rainforest Rescue**		Have the continuous activity come to an end as some of the animals (some counselors could dress up) join in the carnival and interact with campers. Have them sign autographs and tell stories about their lives. End the special event with a big dance complete with several "line"	
12:00	**Animal Crackers**	**Lunch** Theme: Happy Birthday Mother Earth!	**Activities** Throw a party for the planet. Sing Happy Birthday. Have a birthday cake. Have each camper make a wish for the planet or write down what they can do to help the planet and wrap it up as a present. Campers can share these thoughts in their small groups. When you eat the meal try not to use paper.	
1:00	**Crystal Springs**	**All Camp Swimming**	**Riddle of the Day:** Q: Why are fish so smart? A: They swim in schools	
2:30	**Singin' in the Rain**	**Showtime** Clubs and small groups present: Skits Songs	**Counselors' Skit** Slide show: Have counselors present a slide show of their recent trip to the rainforest. Counselors could also do the "Its too darn hot to move" skit.	
3:30 4:00	**Homeward Bound**	**Songs** Singin' in the Rain If I had a Hammer Camper Choice Friends	**Activities** Spirit Sticks Super Safari Group Stamping passports	**Closing Activity** Scientist returns to thank campers and gives them one last tip to save the rain-forests. Plan a tree planting ceremony on camp grounds. Each small group could plant a tree and water it all summer

RAINY DAY
MONSOON MADNESS

9:00 | **All Camp Activities**

- Make a rainforest tape. Have campers create a variety of instruments (drums, horns etc.) and use these instruments to create a musical tape of what a rainforest might sound like in rain, at sunset, sunrise, etc.

- Appropriate video possibilities which compliment the theme include: The Lorax (Dr. Seuss story), Romancing the Stone, Around the World in 80 Days, The Adventures of Huckleberry Finn, Jungle Book, Rici Tici Tavi, Swiss Family Robinson, Robinson Crusoe (original and Walt Disney version), and Castaway Cowboy.

- Crazy Creature Features. Paper bag skits - Each small group is given a paper bag with a dozen props. They must make a crazy creature skit, using all the props in the bag.

- If rain is expected the following day have campers come prepared to take a rain hike and go puddle jumping. If campers have dry clothes to change into, play games in the rain or have a mud olympics. As long as it is not thundering and lightning the rain can create program opportunities, not limit them.

- Organize a dutch auction. Make it a big production. If rain is expected the following day have campers prepare the night before and bring their supplies with them to day camp.

- Hold an indoor nature fair. Display interesting things the campers have found or brought from home. Have groups draw hidden pictures in which they hide animals in the drawings and challenge other groups to find the animals. Be careful that children don't pick up live plants or animals.

2:00 | - Have a backwards day. Reverse the order of the day. Have closing activites first and opening activities last. Have all the campers wear their clothes backwards. When walking around campers must walk backwards.

Small Group Activities

- Make terrariums from two liter pop bottles. Make animal masks.

- Create a bug zoo. Catch as many insects and critters as you can. Gently place them in containers with air holes. After completing the collection show them to other groups. Treat animals with care and when finished let all the animals go in the same place that you found them.

- Have campers illustrate a book they have read or a book read to the small group. Once groups are done get together and let each small group tell the story through their pictures.

- Have a show and tell time and let campers bring in something from home. Create special theme times when campers would bring in things connected to the theme (i.e. something from the best vacation you ever took).

- Have a board game tournament. Create a lifesize monopoly board and have campers themselves be the playing pieces.

- Set up a beauty parlor, complete with an area for shampooing hair, doing nails and facials, and putting on make-up.

4:00 | - Have a dress up meal. Each camper should make a costume. At lunch have other campers guess each animal.

APPENDIX III

VISUALIZING THE PROGRAM/EVENT

VISUALIZING THE PROGRAM/EVENT

Title of Program:

Overview of Program:

The purpose of this program is for youth to learn more about. . .

When youth learn more about. . . they will be more. . .

Types of Activities:

The activities within this program are intended to. . .

They include the following:

- •
- •
- •

- •
- •
- •

Suggested Number of Participants:

Developmental Needs Met by Program:

Youth development competencies and needs that will be addressed are. . .

Conclusion/Wrap-up:

Safety Precautions:

Follow-up Activities:

Resources:

BIBLIOGRAPHY

ACA (1984). *Camping Standards with Interpretations.* Martinsville, IN: American Camping Association.

Albrecht, K. and R. Zemke (1985). *Service America!* Homewood, IL: Dow Jones-Irwin.

Albrecht, K.M. and M.C. Plantz (1991). *Developmentally Appropriate Practice in School-Age Child Care Programs.* Alexandria, VA: American Home Economics Association.

Bloom, B.S. (1956). *Taxonomy of Educational Objectives: Cognitive Domain.* New York: McKay.

Bredekamp, S. (Ed.) (1987). *Developmentally-Appropriate Practice in Early Childhood Programs Serving Children from Birth to Age 8.* Washington, D.C.: National Association for the Education of Young Children.

Bush, P. (1972). *A Program Course for Writing of Performance Objectives.* Chico, CA:North California Program Development Center.

Carnegie Council on Adolescent Development—Task Force on Youth Development and Community Programs (1992). *A Matter of Time: Risk and Opportunity in the Nonschool Hours.* New York: Carnegie Corporation of New York.

Chenary, M. (April, 1985). Toward a More Concrete Understanding of Child Behavior. *Camping Magazine.* p. 26-28.

Csikszentmihalyi, M. (1975). *Beyond Boredom and Anxiety.* San Francisco: Jossey-Bass.

DeGraaf, D.G. and K. DeGraaf (1994). *U.S. Army Youth Services Training Guide: Planning and Supervising Camp Programs* (in press).

Ditter R. (1988). "Today's Child - Tomorrow's Camp." *Camping Magazine.*

Edginton, C. R. and S.R.Edginton (1993). "Total Quality Programming Planning." *Journal of Physical Education, Recreation and Dance*

Edginton, C.R. and Ford, P.F. (1985). *Leadership in Recreation and Leisure Service Organizations.* New York: John Wiley & Sons.

Edginton, S.. (1993). *Camp Adventure™*: A New,Innovative Youth Services Practicum Opportunity. *Renaissance Group Newsletter.* 1(2), p. 9.

Edginton, C. and L.J. Luneckas. "Creating Magic at *Camp Adventure™*." *Parks & Recreation.* 27(11), pp 68-73.

Edginton, C.R. and S. R. Edginton (1992)."The Role of Camp Counselors in Values Development for Youth. *"Camping Magazine.*

Edginton, C.R. , C. J. Hanson and S. R. Edginton (1992). *Leisure Programming: Concepts, Trends and Professional Practice.* Dubuque, IA: Brown and Benchmark.

Edginton, Christopher R. and Susan R. Edginton. Creating Magic the *Camp Adventure*™ Way. *Humanics: The Journal of Leadership for Youth and Human Service.* Winter, 1992. p. 4-7.

Erikson, E. H. (1963) *Childhood and Society.* New York: Norton.

Hoppe, J. (1990). "Creating Ad Appeal for Youth." In Cantrell, J. (1991). *Curriculum Development for Issues Programming.* Washington, D.C.: U.S. Department of Agriculture.

Jennings, L. (1989). "Fordham Institute's Index Documents Steep Decline in Children's and Youth's Social Health Since 1970." *Education Week.*

Jordan, D.J. (1992). "Risk Management Guidelines." *Journal of Physical Education, Recreation and Dance.* Cedar Falls, IA: University of Northern Iowa.

Koch, S. (1992). *Using Conflict Resolution to Promote a Peaceful Environment.* Cedar Falls, IA: University of Northern Iowa.

Krathwohl, D. R. (1964). *Taxonomy of Educational Objectives: Affective Domain.* New York: McKay.

Kwak, C. (1992). *Adolescent Time Use and Its Implications for Youth Serving Agencies.* St. Paul, MN: National Youth Leadership Council.

Lewin, K., R. Lippitt and R. White (1939). "Patterns of Aggressive Behavior in Experimentally Created Social Climates." *Journal of Social Psychology.*

Mueller, C. and Webber, M. (1990). *Celebrating Diversity: A Manual for Bringing Multicultural Education to Youth Work.* St. Louis, MO: Anti-Defamation League.

National Commission on the Role of the School and the Community in Improving Adolescent Health. (1990). *Code Blue: Uniting for Healthier Youth.* Alexandria, VA: National Association of State Boards of Education.

Ooms,T. and L. Herendeen (1989). *Adolescent Substance Abuse Treatment: Evolving Policy at Federal, State and City Levels.* Washington, D.C.: Family Impact Seminar, American Association for Marriage and Family Therapy.

Pittman, K.J. (1991). *Promoting Youth Development: Strengthening the Role of Youth Serving and Community Organizations.* New York: Center for Youth Development and Policy Research.

Pittman, K.J. and M. Wright (1991). *A Rationale for Enhancing the Role of the Non-School Voluntary Sector in Youth Development.* New York: Center for Youth Development and Policy Research.

Purpel, D. and K. Ryan (1976). *Moral Education: It Comes With the Territory.* Berkeley, CA: McCutcheon Publishing Corporation.

Scales, P. (1991). A *Portrait of Youth Adolescents in the 1990s.* Carborro, N.C.: Center for Early Adolescence.

Timmer, S.G., J. Eccles, and I. O'Brian (1985). In F.T. Juster and F.B. Stafford (Eds.), *Time, Goods and Well-Being.* Ann Arbor: University of Michigan, Institute for Social Research.

Walton, M. (1988). *The Deming Management Model.* New York: Perigee.

GLOSSARY

Accident Report. This form should be filled out any time first aid is applied (including cleaning and/or application of a band-aid for a simple cut or scrape). Copies of all accident reports should be submitted to the organization's director and should be filed and kept for several years. It is a good policy to call the parent whenever an accident has happened (no matter how small) and tell them what happened and the treatment administered. A sample accident report is included in the Appendix.

Affective Development. The Affective Domain of development involves feelings, values and emotions. The Affective Domain of learning may involve an attitudinal change, an appreciation or the development of an interest. In terms of the Affective Domain, learners may (1) merely receive or become aware of the existence of an attitude; (2) respond as a result of that awareness; (3) value the particular attitude, interest or appreciation; (4) organize the attitude or interest into a value system; or (5) internalize the attitude, interest or appreciation so that it becomes a positive characteristic of behavior.

Age Appropriateness. The term age appropriateness means that programs and activities correspond to the reliable processes and stages of growth and change that occur in youth. Age appropriateness also has been referred to as "stage" appropriateness.

Anticipatory Planning. Learning how to anticipate needs in advance and meet them before they are requested. Anticipatory planning requires the leader to think in advance (days, weeks months), to visualize services as they will likely unfold, and anticipate actions that may be needed.

Attention to Detail. Success in youth programs is painted in small steps as well as broad strokes. The little things done to make a program of higher quality make the difference between superior services and mediocre ones.

Authoritarian Leader. The leader makes all the decisions. The leader usually dictates the particular task for each group member.

Autonomy. Providing for opportunities for self-direction within activities. For example, allowing youths to develop their own skit which may deviate from what staff envisioned or adapting rules of a game to fit the youths' needs or desires.

Bag of Tricks. Youth leaders need to develop a "bag of tricks" to be used during lulls in programs, and when something unexpected happens. A bag of tricks includes a "kit" of games, songs, puzzles, riddles, jokes, magic tricks, crafts and activity cards, that he/she can use on the spur of the moment.

Basic Needs of Youth. Youth have certain basic needs that must be met that are fundamental for survival and healthy development: A need for positive social interaction; a need for safety, structure and clear limits; a need for belonging and meaningful involvement in family, school, community; need for creative expression; a need for feeling self-worth/giving to others; a need for physical activity; a need to feel a sense of independence, autonomy and control; a need for closeness in relationships; a need for feeling a sense of competence and achievement; a need for a sense of individualism, identity, and self-definition.

Cafeteria Approach. The leader using this approach offers several different programs and services, and lets kids pick from among them.

Child Abuse. Child abuse takes many forms and includes physical abuse, emotional/verbal abuse, sexual abuse and neglect.

Citizenship Competency (ethics and preparation). Youth need to understand their *nation's and community's history and values,* and *desire to contribute* to nation and community.

Cognitive Domain. Cognitive development is related to those processes by which youth think, know and gain an awareness of objects and events. In terms of cognitive development, the youth leader will need to determine whether the learner will (1) merely possess the knowledge, (2) understand it, (3) analyze it, (4) apply it, (5) synthesize it with other knowledge, or (6) evaluate it.

Cognitive/Creative Competence. Youth need to develop a broad base of *knowledge*, ability to appreciate/participate in areas of *creative expression*, good oral, written *language skills, problem-solving and analytical skills*, ability to learn/*interest in learning and achieving*.

Combined Approach. As the name suggests, this approach recommends using any one or more of the above approaches depending on the circumstances.

Community Needs Survey. A community needs survey is a more general survey of community needs that is distributed to adults; however, it may contain a section on the needs and activities of youth.

Conflict Resolution. There are processes that can be used, specifically the 2x4 method of conflict resolution, that offer a quick and positive way to resolve relatively simple problems, which have not been simmering for a long period of time, between a leader and a child, <u>or</u> between two children.

Content Areas. There are specific content areas that youth leaders can incorporate into their programs. By using a number of content areas, the youth leader is able to offer a variety of programs that will meet various needs of youth. Content areas include active games, aquatics, crafts, drama, initiative games, low organized games, music, nature, New Games, rainy day, special events and sports.

Continuous Education. Good people make good programs, but the needs of youth are dynamic and changing, requiring continuous education and development. Youth leaders should seek ways to improve their knowledge base.

Continuous Improvement. The best way to achieve quality is to improve the processes associated with creating youth services. Constantly searching out new ways of doing things better, more cost efficiently and/or in a way that is more meaningful to youth. Establishing a goal of making one small change in every program every week to improve the quality.

Current Practice Approach. The leader follows the latest trends as a basis for program ideas, as well as what is going on in other organizations currently.

Democratic Leader. The leader attempts to build group consensus on all decisions made by the group. All policies are a matter of group discussion and decision, encouraged and assisted by the leader.

Developmental Competencies. Five basic areas of youth development competencies have been developed based on a review of the youth development areas that are seen as being important by youth-serving organizations. They are health/physical competence, personal/social competence, cognitive/creative competence, vocational competence, and citizenship competency.

Developmentally-Appropriate Programming. Developmentally appropriate programs are tailored to the developmental characteristics and needs of the children and youth they serve. Activities and experiences offered in developmentally-appropriate school-age programs contribute to all aspects of a youth's development. It is important that the youth leader consider not only the age appropriateness of activities, but also the individual-appropriateness.

Entrepreneurship. The youth leader may be able to add to existing resources by using creative strategies. "Entrepreneurial" strategies that the leader may use to expand program opportunities at no extra cost include scrounging, collaboration/cooperation, sponsorships, gifts and donations and involvement of constituents.

Evaluation. Evaluation is used to measure how well the leader and the organization achieve the goals and objectives of program(s) that have been set. It measures the difference between goals and outcome, expectations and results. It includes two activities: 1) formative evaluation, which deals with evaluating the program as it is still taking place and making corrections; and 2) summative evaluation, which involves evaluation of the program after it is over and then making recommendations for future programs.

Exceeding Expectations. Providing services that *exceed what customers have asked for* or have paid for is the goal of the leader. If the leader does not accomplish this goal (exceed expectations), customers will view the program or service only as adequate or less than adequate.

Expressed Desires Approach. This approach involves use of surveys and other similar material as a basis for program planning.

Formative Evaluation. Ongoing, or *formative evaluation* is carried on throughout the program. In other words, the youth leader evaluates the program as it is going on, and then makes corrections necessary to improve the program as it is in process. For example, youth may provide feedback that indicates that the program is not meeting their expectations, at which point the leader may evaluate the situation and restructure the activity.

Health/Physical Competence. Youth need to have *good current health status* and appropriate knowledge, attitudes and *behaviors to ensure future health* (exercise, good diet, nutrition).

Incident Report. This form should be filled out to document any incident that takes place at camp. Incidents are any situations that are out of the ordinary at camp and includes such things as missing youth, suspected child abuse, fighting, thefts, etc. As with accident reports, all incident reports should be submitted to that organization's director and should be kept on file for several years.

Individual Appropriateness. Individual appropriateness refers to the fact that it is important for the youth leader to be sensitive and responsive to the pattern of growth of each individual youth. Individual appropriateness is an important consideration, since youth can be the same age, yet be at different levels developmentally in terms of mastery of skills.

Initial Planning. In the initial planning step of the program planning process, the youth leader focuses on two activities: 1) determining what resources and facilities are available for programs; and 2) attempting to determine the needs of youth by involving youth in planning, assessing the needs of youth, and review of written material in the area of youth development competencies and needs.

Innovation.   Success in youth programming stems from a commitment to innovation. Programs should constantly evolve to meet the needs of children and youth. Innovative organizations constantly look for new and different services, equipment, areas and facilities that improve the quality of services to youth.

Laissez-Faire Leader. The leader allows the group total freedom to make decisions. Complete nonparticipation by the leader in the group process.

Life Stages of Youth.   One concept of youth development has been developed by psychologist Erik Erikson. He indicates that youth (as well as adults) progress through eight life stages related to personality development and that within each stage they establish new orientations to themselves and other people in their social world. At each life stage youth need to master a new level of social interaction, and as this process takes place their personality can be changed either positively or negatively. Erikson says that youth need to achieve competency, a personal identity, and a feeling of closeness or intimacy with others within this process.

Needs Assessment. Needs assessment, as the name suggests, is a process for gathering information regarding the needs and wants of youth, and then using this information to select and set priorities for program planning that meet youths' needs. Once youths' needs are identified, the youth leader evaluates them in terms of the values of the organization and the degree to which it has the resources to provide the desired services.

Negligence. In order to prove negligence, four elements must exist, including duty owed, breach of duty, resulting accident, and actual damages incurred.

Objectives Approach.   The leader using this approach sets performance and/or learning objectives that specify outcomes expected from program participation.

Organizational Assessment. Prior to program development and during the initial phase of planning, the leader must determine what resources are available for programs and activities, including areas and facilities, supplies, equipment, staff and other resources. This will determine the support that is available for programs.

Perceived Competence. "Perceived competence" means that the leader designs programs so that youth are faced with *challenges that are at a level equal to their ability*, so that they can achieve success and feel "competent."

Perceived Freedom. "Perceived freedom" means that the leader creates opportunities for youth to choose from a variety of different activities, giving them the illusion (or reality) of *freedom of choice*.

Performance Measurements. The youth leader can progress toward achievement of quality by creating performance measurements. Participant numbers, youth outcomes related to performance measures, program costs, participant use hours, participant survey results are all sources of data for charts to measure performance. Measuring achievement over a period of time, enables the youth leader to see gains in quality and performance, and to justify future program developments.

Performance/Learning Objectives for Youth. Whatever it is that the leader wants youth to accomplish as a result of participating in a program, must be written out in terms of objectives in a very specific way following certain guidelines. This is done so that the leader may later evaluate whether the objectives that were set have been achieved. Such guidelines must be specific, measurable, reality-based, useful and linked to youth needs.

Personal/Social Competence. It is important that youth gain *intrapersonal skills* (ability to understand personal emotions, have self-discipline); *interpersonal skills* (ability to work with others, develop friendships and relationships through communication, cooperation, empathizing, negotiating); *coping/system skills* (ability to adapt, assume responsibility); and *judgment skills* (plan, make decisions, solve problems).

Prescriptive Approach. This approach is most commonly used in the therapeutic recreation setting, often to respond to dysfunctional behavior.

Pride. Belief in what you are doing is contagious. Pride is having a high opinion of yourself and your work. Pride comes from doing a job competently as well as having ownership in the effort.

Program Development. Within the program development step of the planning process, the youth leader will focus on selecting the program area, specific type of program, program format, facilities, setting, equipment and supplies, staffing, cost, promotion and risk management.

Program Formats. There are various ways that the youth leader can offer and arrange programs and services for youth. These are often called *"program formats."* The leader can also use organizational formats such as competitive, drop-in/open, class, club, retreats, special events and outreach.

Program Objectives. It is important for the youth leader to identify program goals and objectives. What is it that the youth leader hopes to see youth accomplish as a result of participation in programs and activities? In addition, specific behavioral objectives may be written that outline the particular physical behaviors that youth will exhibit as a result of participation.

Program Promotion. Program promotion is geared toward informing participants about programs, activities and events, as well as representing the organization to the public and higher officials in such a way that financial support is maintained or enhanced. Use of the media, brochures, flyers and other tools, help the leader promote program offerings and attract youth to participate in them.

Program Quality. Quality is not just measured by numbers of participants or meeting the break-even cost of a program; it is also measured in the reaction of participants, the way in which a program unfolds, the degree to which youth develop and meet their needs, and the extent to which youth genuinely, enthusiastically, and meaningfully experience leisure.

Progression in Activities. A progression of skills based on ability, age and/or experience must be incorporated into the program in order to meet the needs of youths.

Psychomotor/Physical Development. The Psychomotor Domain of development includes the acquisition of physical and neuromuscular skills. In terms of psychomotor skills, youth progress from imitation, to manipulation, to precision, to articulation and naturalization. The Psychomotor Domain is the skill domain involving movement. The acts of playing ball, writing and speaking are examples of learning in this domain.

Quality Measurement. Quality is measured by whether the organization achieves the requirements that have been established for serving youth. Quality, then, is the conformance to requirements, standards, policies, or procedures that have been set by the organization.

Risk Management Plans. It is important for staff to develop ways to manage risk associated with programs. *A risk management plan is a tool for identifying and controlling the risk or hazards while maximizing the camps' effectiveness with youth.* The objectives of a risk management plan are threefold. First, to provide a safe environment for campers and staff. Second, to anticipate potential hazards and problem situations and plan for them. Third, to provide a plan to follow in crisis situations, thus protecting staff and the program from accusations of negligence.

Risk. A risk is an uncertainty or probability concerning the loss of resources. In a camp setting, these resources may be individual youth or staff members, or the facility itself.

Social Health. Social health includes such factors as success in school, being substance-free, and other behaviors in accordance with social mores.

Staff Journals. Accident and incident reports can be incorporated into some kind of youth center journal where staff keep a running dialogue of what is happening each day. Such a journal can be used to record such things as when medications are given out, when a youth is picked up early, when certain youth are having behavior problems, reminders to staff, etc.

Standard of Care. When asked to decide if a staff member is negligent in a certain situation, the courts will compare the action of the staff member to a reasonably prudent person. *For youth leaders, the courts will hold them to the level of a care of a professional, college educated, youth leader.* The actual way that appropriate behavior is most commonly judged by the courts is through the opinions of experts in the field, the written standards of the profession, or both.

Summative Evaluation. Final or summative evaluation occurs at the end of the program as a final wrap-up. This type of evaluation attempts to review the entire program, consider its strengths and weaknesses, and then make final judgment on the impact it achieved, the degree to which it met its goals and recommendations for future programs.

Teaming. The Total Quality approach is dependent upon team-work, cooperation and supportive behavior. All staff should be focused and have their eyes and efforts directed toward the *primary goal*, which is providing the very highest quality services for youth, and staff should be willing to do what it takes to make that happen.

Total Quality Program Planning (TQP). TQP is based on the assumption that the leader can work within the organization to produce quality leisure programs that consistently and effectively meet the needs of youth and exceed their expectations. It relies on customer service, principles of youth development and programming based on youth involvement.

Traditional Approach. The leader depends on what has been done in past years for program ideas.

Types of Leadership Style. Three basic types of leadership have been identified and include authoritarian, democratic and laissez-faire.

Value Clarification. There are a number of statements that can be used by the leader to help youth think about and clarify their values. *These statements can be used to talk to youth in a brief, thought-provoking manner* so that they begin to focus more clearly on who they are, what they believe in and what they want to do. For example, "Have you felt this way for a long time?" "Is that very important to you?" and others.

Value Clarifying Guidelines. As the leader uses value clarifying statements, there are guidelines that should be adhered to. For example "There are no right answers." "The responsibility is on the youth to examine his/her values," and others.

Values Development. Values development is *based on the idea that the leader can help youth develop and define their values through use of selected methods.*

Values. Values are *principles or guidelines that individuals believe to be important in life.* Values are freely chosen after some consideration and, once developed, are acted upon. Very often, values determine the course of action that an individual will take, and will influence the way in which they direct their energy and resources.

Visualizing Programs. The leader engaged in planning should *mentally visualize any program, activity or event* from the time the youth enter it until they leave.

Vocational Competence. It is important for youth to develop a broad understanding/*awareness of vocational (and avocational) options* and of steps to act on choices; adequate preparation for career, understanding of value and function of work/leisure.

Youth Development Objectives. Youth-serving agencies have purposes and objectives for the work they do. Youth-serving organizations that are committed to youth development all have youth development objectives, toward which they focus their efforts.

Youth Leadership/Ownership. The leader can interact with youths in ways that will foster a sense of ownership. This can be assisted by providing choice, flexibility, autonomy, and progression in activities.

Youth Needs Survey and Report. A youth needs survey provides information regarding the types of activities that youth currently participate in, the frequency of participation, activities that youth would like to participate in if available, as well as other questions related to youth and their problems and needs.

Youth Ownership/Empowerment. Rather than have the staff plan <u>for</u> youth, the leader should *draw in youth to help in the planning and execution of programs,* activities and events.

Annual Reports. Annual Reports contain information regarding current and eligible users of youth services. This information can be used to help provide a basis for planning.

Youth-Centered Program Planning Process. The "Youth-Centered" Program Planning diagram or model has six (6) steps, including preparation, initial planning, program goals and objectives, program design/program format, program implementation, and evaluation.